YES! THERE IS A GOLDMINE IN BUFFALO

The right way to invest in section 8

Syed Mukit Ahmed

CONTENTS

WHY SHOULD YOU READ THIS BOOK?

Unveiling Hidden Treasures: This book is more than just an investing guide; it's a revelation of Buffalo's undiscovered treasure in the Section 8 housing market.

Knowledge at Your Fingertips: Syed Ahmed, a seasoned investor, presents tried-and-true strategies for success in the dynamic Buffalo real estate market in this book.

Data-Driven Insights: Armed with the most recent market data and trends, you'll obtain a thorough understanding of how to navigate and prosper in this one-of-a-kind market.

Make a Difference: Discover how your investments may benefit communities by combining financial success with social responsibility.

Beyond Real Estate: This book is about developing entrepreneurial abilities and changing your financial perspective, not just property investing.

"Yes! There is a Goldmine in Buffalo" is more than just a real estate book. It's an invitation to join the ranks of astute investors who realize Buffalo's market potential. This book is your necessary guide if you're ready to explore a wealth of chances and make a lasting difference.

My name is Syed Mukit Ahmed. I am a seasoned software engineer living in Milwaukee, WI, as well as a visionary real estate investor specializing in Section 8 housing. My path, as detailed in "Yes! There is a Goldmine in Buffalo," involves more than just financial triumph. It's an enlightening story of empathy, perseverance, and empowerment that combines my desire for investment with a deep dedication to effective real estate investment.

My upbringing in Bangladesh, where I was born into a middle-class, broken family, was fraught with difficulties, particularly in finding safe shelter. My mother's unrelenting fortitude and determination affected this period of my life tremendously. She worked diligently to support us as a single mother, instilling in me the qualities of perseverance and adaptation. Her sacrifices and hard labor were the foundation of my journey, which culminated in my important migration to the United States, a move that altered my life and instilled in me a spirit of tenacity. In addition, my wife's steadfast support was a pillar in our path. Her constant presence and support were crucial, especially during our relocation to the United States and the subsequent obstacles. She was a continual source of strength for me, and she never let me down.

My studies at the University of Dhaka, a center for excellent business education, sparked an interest in diversifying investments across several asset classes. My venture into the stock market, particularly ETF funds, demonstrated my financial acumen. However, it was my strategic foray into real estate, particularly Section 8 investments supported by US government rents, that defined my investment journey. This move demonstrates my ability to combine academic knowledge with practical investment methods that target safe, high-yielding possibilities.

While living in Milwaukee, WI, I began a mission-driven real estate investing enterprise in Buffalo, NY. My strategy goes beyond monetary considerations to develop communities, ensure tenant safety, and make a beneficial societal impact. My properties are more than just structures; they are havens of hope and joy.

As a landlord, I see homes as safe havens for making treasured experiences. This viewpoint has altered the traditional landlord-tenant dynamic into a caring and understanding one.

My book serves as a guide for prospective Section 8 property investors. It's a collection of my sympathetic investment strategies, experiences, and philosophy, with the goal of promoting sustainable and socially responsible property investment.

My life narrative, from the streets of Bangladesh to the USA's real estate market, is a source of inspiration. It highlights investment's dual potential for profit and social effect, encouraging people to use real estate as a tool for positive change.

CHAPTER 1
Understanding Section 8 Investment
How to Start Investing in Real Estate

Hello, and welcome to the world of opportunity!
It might seem scary to invest in real estate if you've never done it before. You may have heard of mutual funds, stocks, and bonds as ways to trade, but real estate, especially Section 8 investing, is a whole new level. You can start reading this chapter to learn why Section 8 properties in Buffalo, NY, are a great investment opportunity for both new and experienced investors.

Not only is this book a help, but it's also a way to learn about one of the best ways to invest in real estate that isn't being used enough. These pages are meant to help you learn how to invest in Section 8 housing in a way that is both profitable and moral, no matter how much experience you have or how new you are to investing.

Section 8 offers benefits like guaranteed rent, government subsidies, and stable, long-term tenancies.

The world of Section 8 housing investing is always changing, and people don't always understand it. Buffalo, NY, offers a unique environment for people who want to invest in this area. The goal of this book is to make investing in Section 8 homes in this area less mysterious and shed light on the many benefits of Section 8 investments. These include guaranteed rent percentages, on-time direct deposits from the government, and regular property checks that protect your capital.

Buffalo's Section 8 market offers distinctive opportunities and is subject to strict regulations like many others. For example, Buffalo is a good place for Section 8 investments because there is a need for affordable homes there and the city's economy is doing well. This book will help you understand how the local market works, why it's important to build a strong support system, and how to deal with the Section 8 program's complicated rules and relationships between landlords and tenants.

We will also talk about ways to find homes that will make money, how to manage them well, and how to make sure that tenants stay for a long time, which is a key part of successful Section 8 investing. This book combines local knowledge with general Section 8 investment ideas to give you the skills and confidence to start or grow your investment portfolio in Buffalo's Section 8 housing market, turning problems into chances to make money.

When it comes to real estate, Section 8 property is a one-of-a-kind chance that combines doing good for others with making money. This book is based on a lot of experience and information, including the advice of experts in the field and personal stories. It's designed to take the mystery out of Section 8 investments by giving you the information and tools you need to make smart choices. I can articulate the key benefits of Section 8 as follows:

- **Guaranteed Rent Payments:** Section 8 programs often guarantee rent payments, which gives owners a steady stream of income.

- **Regular Government Subsidies:** The government subsidizes a big chunk of the rent, which makes sure that payments are made on time and lowers the risk of not paying the rent.

- **Diverse Tenant Pool:** You can choose from a larger group of possible renters, which can be especially helpful in places where Section 8 housing is in high demand.

- **Low Vacancy Rates:** Because there is a high desire for affordable housing, Section 8 properties often have lower vacancy rates than other rental properties.

- **Tax Incentives:** There may be a number of tax benefits and incentives that come with building affordable homes.

- **A contribution to social good** is that investing in Section 8 housing helps the community by giving low-income families good homes.

- **Long-term Tenancies:** A lot of Section 8 tenants like long-term leases because they give landlords more security and lower turnover costs.

- **Property Maintenance Standards:** The housing authority inspects homes on a regular basis to make sure they are well-kept and keep their value.

- **Demand Rises During Economic Downturns:** Demand for Section 8 housing often rises during economic downturns, which makes the market more stable.

- **Potential for Appreciation:** Much like any other real estate investment, Section 8 homes could go up in value over time.

The pages that follow will take you on a thorough journey through the pros and cons of being a Section 8 owner. Everything is talked about in detail, from the guaranteed income streams and the joy of helping the community to following government rules and keeping up with property standards. There are two sides to every story, and this book tries to show the truth about what it means to invest in Section 8 homes.

It's not just about making money in the world of Section 8 housing; it's also about adding value for both owners and the people they serve. This book will help you find your way through the complicated parts of market research, dealing with tenants, property management, and the moral issues that come up when working in this field.

As you read these pages, get ready for your ideas to be tested and your knowledge to grow. There's more to this book than just instructions; it shows how Section 8 housing can be a key part of your business portfolio. Welcome to the trip, and let's open the doors to a world of possibilities in investing in Section 8 housing.

What is Section 8?

Section 8, also known as the Housing Choice Voucher Program, is a federal program that helps low-income families, the elderly, and people with disabilities pay for housing. The program provides housing vouchers to help with rental costs. In most real estate investments, landlords get rent straight from tenants. With Section 8, however, landlords get most, if not all, of their rent from the government. This means steady and stable income, which is a big plus for investors.

Why is Section 8 used in Buffalo, NY?

The real estate market in Buffalo offers a one-of-a-kind chance. The prices of homes here are lower than in many other U.S. cities, which makes the original investment less scary. Plus, because it's in New York State, residents and investors can take advantage of some of the best state-level housing aid programs.

The Call for People Who Aren't Investors
Buffalo is a great place to invest in real estate if you've never thought about it before.

- **Stable Income:** The government-backed rent ensures a constant flow of income, reducing the likelihood that tenants won't pay.

- **Growing Market:** The market in Buffalo is going up, which means that the money you spend today could be worth a lot more tomorrow.

- **Supportive Environment:** Section 8 takes away a lot of the guessing and risk that come with being a landlord. This is because the program is well organized and the caseworkers are helpful.

New York is one of the greatest states, which has benefits both for investors and for tenants

Putting Myths to Rest
Some people have the wrong idea about Section 8; they think it's too hard, too risky, or only for experts. The goal of this book is to dispel these myths and show that Section 8 trading can be easy and profitable for everyone, even those who have never done it before.

This is where your journey begins
This book will help you understand the possibilities of Section 8 investments in Buffalo, NY, whether you're an experienced investor or just interested in real estate. We'll talk about the pros

and cons, clear up any confusion, and start you on the path to a smart and profitable investment trip. Its goal is to take the mystery out of Section 8 investing and show it as an easy-to-reach and appealing chance, based on solid data and personal insights.

Final thought

As this chapter on Section 8 real estate investments comes to a close, let's look forward to the next one with hope and drive. Section 8 housing in Buffalo, NY, is more than just a way to make money. It's also a way to make a difference and secure financial growth. The foundation has been built in this chapter, which has shown you the unique benefits and cleared up some common misconceptions. You are now ready to succeed. Remember that putting money into Section 8 is more than just a choice; it's a commitment to community growth and proof of how powerful smart, moral investing can be. You're not just learning about business strategies as you read these pages; you're also opening the door to a world where making money and doing good are both possible. As you start this exciting trip, let this book be your guide, your teacher, and your source of inspiration. Let's work together to turn problems into chances and dreams into reality. You are now in the world of Section 8 real estate investment. This is where you can be an entrepreneur and make a change that lasts.

CHAPTER 2
What's so great about Buffalo? A Look at the Market

Buffalo, New York, is more than just a dot on a map. Welcome to the heart of the city. Modernity and history mix perfectly there; the sounds of a rich past meet the lively beat of a bright future. This chapter isn't just about numbers and statistics; it's about finding a hidden gem in the real estate world, a market brimming with potential and opportunity.

Buffalo, a city that has been through storms and come out better, is a great example of how to be strong and grow. It's not just cheap to live in that city; it's also a place where real estate ownership and smart investing goals can come true. As we learn more about Buffalo's real estate market, we find that it's a great place to spend time and explore, especially when it comes to Section 8 housing.

There is more to this chapter than just analysis. It's a walk through the streets of Buffalo that looks at the unique possibilities that this market offers. So come learn why Buffalo isn't just another city— why it's a beacon for smart investors and a haven for real estate investors looking for a mix of security and growth.

Buffalo, New York, is a strong city that

*blends history and modernity, and its
real estate market is full of opportunities
and growth for smart investors.*

As we turn each page, we'll learn more about Buffalo's market, from its roots in the past to its present trends. We will talk about why this city is a goldmine for those who know where to look, even though it is often missed. It's not just about buying homes; it's also about investing in a community, a place that's growing, and a future that shines as brightly as Niagara Falls.

Let's go on this trip together and look at the streets, numbers, and stories that make Buffalo's real estate market a treasure waiting to be found. Welcome to Buffalo, where chances meet stability, history meets promise, and your journey as an investor starts here.

As we go on, we'll get into the details of Buffalo's real estate market and look at what makes it a good choice for investors, especially those who want to buy Section 8 housing. We'll look at the market trends, the cost, the investment possibilities, and the housing demand from the point of view of an investor who sees past the surface. Join us as we look into the real value of Buffalo's real estate market, which offers not only the chance to make money but also to make a positive difference in a city that is growing.

A Short History of Buffalo
Buffalo is a city in the western part of New York State. It has a long past and a bright future. Buffalo is a beautiful city known for its rich culture, historic architecture, and closeness to Niagara Falls. But it's also a growing center for the real estate business.

How is the real estate market in Buffalo right now?
There is a lot of stability and room for progress in Buffalo's real

estate market. When compared to big cities, where the real estate market can be unstable and overvalued, Buffalo is a more stable and approachable place to live. The real estate market in Buffalo is a mix of stability and promise, with home prices steadily going up and a steady demand. Some recent data peaks are:

- **Typical home prices:**
  In September 2023, the Buffalo, NY, real estate market offered investors and renters an interesting situation. The average price of a house in the city was around $202,000. This number illustrates the modest but noticeable increase of 1.0% from this point last year. The small but steady rise in home prices shows that the market is solid and slowly appreciating, which means that there is a healthy demand for housing in the area.

  There are several reasons for this steady rise in home prices. To begin, Buffalo's economy may have gone through some good changes, like more jobs or better infrastructure, which may have led to a higher desire for housing. The city may also be attracting more buyers because it is a cheaper choice than New York's more expensive markets. These buyers may include first-time homeowners and investors interested in Section 8 properties.

  Also, the 1.0% year-over-year rise is especially important for buyers to think about when they look at the bigger picture of the economy. In a world where many real estate markets are very unstable or have growth rates that are too high, Buffalo's market has a more stable and long-term growth trend. Investors who like safety and predictability are often more interested in this type of market behavior than rapid growth that might not last.

Buffalo's real estate market has steady growth and healthy demand, making it a stable and promising place to invest in Section 8

These numbers are very important for Section 8 owners. Buffalo has pretty reasonable home prices, which makes it a good place to buy rental houses. The steady rise in home values also means that investments in this market are likely to go up in value over time. This means that investors can get steady rental income and possibly big capital gains.

To sum up, the average home price in Buffalo in September 2023 shows that the real estate market is steady and slowly rising in value. This trend is good news for investors, especially those interested in Section 8 housing, because it means that initial investments will be reasonable and property values will likely rise over time. Data Source

- **Median Listing and Sale Prices:**
The usual listing price of homes in Buffalo, NY, in the second quarter of 2023 was $133,000. This showed that the market was strong and changing quickly. However, this is only the beginning of the story. The typical sale price, which went up to $150,000, is the more important number. The fact that the sale price is so much higher than the listing price shows that there is a lot of desire in the market.

When there is such a big difference between the list price and the sale price, it usually means that homes are selling, and they're selling in a competitive market. People are ready to pay more than the asking price, which means there is more demand than supply in the market. During this situation, there are often bidding wars where many people want to buy the same property, which drives up the end price.

This trend is especially interesting for investors and people who want to buy a house. For investors, it means the market is healthy and there is a chance for capital growth and a good return on investment. Given that sale prices are going up, homes bought at the current market rates are expected to go up in value. For people who want to buy a home, this trend shows how important it is to act quickly because prices are likely to keep going up, making cost a bigger issue.

A growing population, stable economic conditions, or a lack of available homes for sale are just a few of the factors contributing to this change in prices. Understanding these underlying reasons is important for anyone who wants to invest in or buy property in the area because it shows how long this market trend will last.

In short, the big difference between the typical listing price and sale price in Buffalo's real estate market in the second quarter of 2023 shows how much people want to live there. Different people in the market are facing both chances and challenges in this situation, which makes it an exciting time to be in the Buffalo real estate market. Data Source

- **Comparative Market Trends:**
An increase in the average home price is a strong sign of a healthy and resilient market. That means that the Buffalo real estate market is not only keeping its value but also growing steadily, even though there are economic pressures from outside sources, like inflation or changes in interest rates. Investors who want to put their money into markets that are going to go up a lot will really like this kind of growth.

A rise like this can make investors feel better about their money. It means that homes in Buffalo are getting more valuable, which could mean that they are good investments. This could mean higher property values over time for people who invest in Section 8 housing. This could mean bigger cash gains if they decide to sell in the future.

Home prices usually go up when there is a lot of desire for homes in the area. Many things could be to blame for this, such as population growth, economic growth, or a lack of homes. A market with a lot of demand can mean lower vacancy rates and a larger group of potential tenants for Section 8 investors.

As for economic indicators, rising home prices can also be a sign of a healthy economy in the area as a whole. It could mean that there are more jobs, higher wages, or other economic activities that make the place better off overall. For real estate investors, this economic stability is very important because it has a direct effect on the rental market and people's ability to afford homes.

Home prices have been going up steadily, which suggests that buying property in Buffalo could be a good long-term investment. It shows that the market isn't just going through a short-term surge but is actually growing steadily, which is important for making long-term investments.

With home prices going up, the real estate market in Buffalo offers a unique mix of affordability and and long-term business potential.

Buffalo's market has an advantage over others where home prices are either staying the same or going down. This could bring in buyers who want to put their money into markets that are growing.

To sum up, the fact that Buffalo's average home prices went up by 5.1% is a strong sign of a healthy and growing real estate market. This growth is good news for investors, both present and potential. It means that real estate investments, especially in the Section 8 housing sector, are likely to be safe and make money. Data Source

- **Affordability:**
Buffalo, New York, stands out in the national real estate market because its home prices are so much lower. Especially when compared to big cities like New York City or Los Angeles, where real estate is known for being very pricey, this pricing stands out. First-time buyers like Buffalo because it's easier for them to buy property there than in other cities. This low cost is a big part of lowering the original financial hurdle that many new investors face.

There are more ways that Buffalo's real estate market is cost-effective than just the buying price. In general, Buffalo has a cheaper cost of living than bigger cities. In this case, not only are the homes cheaper to buy, but the continued costs of owning a home, like taxes, insurance, and repairs, are easier to handle. For buyers who are careful not to take on too much debt, this feature is especially appealing.

For buyers of Section 8 properties, this low cost means a one-of-a-kind chance. When property prices go down, buyers may be able to buy more or bigger properties with the same amount of money they would need in a market where prices were higher. This can help you build a diverse portfolio that spreads risk and raises the chance of making money.

Also, the low cost of homes in Buffalo can mean a higher return on investment (ROI). Because the prices are lower, the yield on investment sites can be very high, but the government subsidizes the rent, which is frequently comparable to market rates. This is a very important point for buyers who want to make the most of their money and get rich over time.

Also, Buffalo's real estate market is very affordable, which makes it a great place for long-term investments. As the city grows and more people move there, investors can take advantage of the chance that property values will go up. This possibility for long-term growth, along with the immediate benefits of Section 8 rental income, makes this an attractive investment opportunity.

In conclusion, Buffalo's real estate market has a unique mix of low prices, a lower cost of living, and the potential for a high return on investment (ROI). This makes it a great place for first-time investors to start and a smart choice for experienced investors. Because of the way the city's market works, there is a unique chance to get into real estate investing with less money and still have the chance to make a lot of money and help people.

- **Potential for Investment:**
The economy in Buffalo is growing and getting better right now. A slow but consistent flow of new people looking for affordable housing, more businesses opening, and infrastructure improvements are all signs of this resurgence. For real estate buyers, this growth means a market that is active and where property values may go up. As the city grows and more people move there, there will likely be a

greater need for housing, including Section 8 homes. This can cause property prices to rise, which can be good for investors who want to make money.

One of the best things about buying in Buffalo's real estate market is that it's not too hard to get started. The costs of homes in Buffalo are much lower than those in bigger cities like New York City or San Francisco. This makes the market accessible to buyers, especially those who are new to real estate or don't have a lot of money. They can get in without having to make a big initial investment, which is usually needed in markets that are more expensive. This is especially good for Section 8 investors because it lets them diversify their investment accounts and lowers the financial risk that comes with buying homes.

Even though Buffalo properties have lower starting investment costs, their values have been going up over time. The need for more homes and the city's expanding economy are contributing factors to this trend. If you invest in Section 8 housing, this means that your money will likely go up in value over time. This is because the government pays for the rent, giving you a steady income. Buffalo is a good place to put your money for the long run because you can get steady rental income and the value of your property may go up.

Buffalo's low cost of living affects more than just the rental market. Buffalo's overall cost of living is lower than the national average. This makes it a good place for families, single people, and people who qualified for Section 8 housing to live. This change in the population can help Section 8 buildings have a stable and growing pool of tenants, which will keep occupancy rates high and lower the risk of vacancies.

In conclusion, Buffalo's real estate market has a unique mix of a growing economy, low startup costs, the chance for property values to rise, and a steady stream of tenants. Because of these things, Section 8 investors can not only make money but also help the community by giving low-income families good housing choices. Because of this, Buffalo is a great place for both experienced and new real estate owners who want to grow their portfolios in a market with a lot of value.

- **Demand for Housing:**
Buffalo, NY's recent surge in population growth is an important thing for real estate owners to think about. A lot of these new people are moving to the area because there are more jobs available. As more businesses open and current ones grow, they bring in workers from other areas, which brings more people to the city. This trend isn't just a short-term rise; it's a steady rise that shows the economy is strong and growing.

As more people move to Buffalo, the need for housing typically rises. This desire isn't just for buying homes; it also includes the rental market, which is why Section 8 investments are so important. There will be a greater need for affordable homes as the population grows. Section 8 properties are useful in this situation because they provide a good option for many new people who are looking for good, low-cost places to live.

Property prices are going up because more people want to live in homes. Homes in Buffalo are likely to get more expensive as more people try to get them. This rise in property prices is good news for investors because it means that buying property in Buffalo now could lead to a big gain in value later on. So, for Section 8 investors, this means that not only can they get stable rental income from government funding, but their investment may also grow in value over time.

In addition, this situation makes the market better for

renters. Due to a lack of accessible homes and more people needing to find homes, landlords may find that their properties are in high demand. If this happens, there may be fewer empty units, and rents may go up, which is good for property owners.

To sum up, Buffalo's growing population and job market are making the city a lively and possibly profitable place for real estate owners. Investing in this area, especially in Section 8 housing, is a good idea because of the rising demand for housing and the chance that property values will go up. As an investor, getting into this growing market could not only make you a lot of money, but it could also help people find homes in a neighborhood that is doing well.

The Case for Investments Under Section 8
The way the market works in Buffalo is especially good for Section 8 investments.

- **Government-Backed Stable Income:** Because the government guarantees rental payments under Section 8, owners have a more stable source of income than with traditional rentals.

- **High Demand for Affordable Housing:** Section 8 homes are a good fit for Buffalo's high demand for affordable housing because they have low vacancy rates and stable renters.

- **Positive Impact on the Community:** Investors who buy Section 8 properties make the community a better place by giving low-income families good housing choices.

- **Different types of properties:** Buffalo's real estate market is very varied, with old houses and new apartments, so there is something for every investor's taste and budget.

Comparative Affordability in the United States

When looking at the U.S. real estate market as a whole, Buffalo stands out because it is affordable and has the potential for high profits.

- **Comparison with Other Big Cities in the U.S.**: Buffalo's average home prices are much lower than those in other great American cities. Because it's easier to get into, this market is great for people who want to start trading but don't have a lot of money to put down at first.

- **Investment Returns**: Even though Buffalo's home prices are lower than those in more expensive markets, the rental rates are still good, and often even better. In this case, the return on investment may be better in Buffalo, especially for Section 8 homes where the government helps pay the rent.

Why is Section 8 important in Buffalo?

Investing in Section 8 homes in Buffalo makes a market that is already very appealing even better.

- **Government-backed security:** Because the government backs the rent, Section 8 investments provide a level of security that isn't always present in other real estate investments.

- **High Demand for Affordable Housing:** People in Buffalo are always looking for affordable housing, which means that Section 8 homes are less likely to become empty.

- **Community Impact:** Investing in Section 8 homes in Buffalo is not only a good way to make money, but it also helps the community by giving people who need it good housing.

Final Thoughts

As this look into Buffalo's real estate market comes to a close, it's clear that this city is more than just a place to spend. It's a living, changing picture that offers a unique mix of stability, affordability, and growth potential. Buffalo is a market that doesn't follow the norm. It has a unique mix of low entry hurdles and high returns, especially when it comes to Section 8 housing.

In this chapter, we've looked at how Buffalo's market has changed over time and how it works now. We've seen that the market is ready for growth and demand because home prices are slowly but steadily going up, and there is a big difference between what homes are listed for and what they sell for. Comparative market trends show that Buffalo is not only holding its own in the face of economic stresses but is also on a path of steady growth. This makes it a good investment for both new and experienced investors.

The real estate market in Buffalo is affordable for more than just the lower prices. It's also accessible for chances that might not be possible in other markets. For Section 8 investors, this means a chance to spread out their holdings, lower their risk, and raise their profits. The city's economy is growing thanks to new businesses and people. This makes it a great place to make investments that are both good for business and good for society.

Putting money into Section 8 housing in Buffalo isn't just about making money; it's also about helping the community, giving people in need good housing, and being a part of a bigger story of urban growth and recovery. It's a bet on a city that's starting a new era in its past, one where public service and economic growth go hand in hand.

Finally, don't forget that the real estate market in Buffalo is more than just numbers and trends. This story shows how strong people can be, how resilient the city is, and how there are opportunities for those who are willing to look deeper. Whether you're an experienced owner or this is your first time buying property, Buffalo has a unique environment where your money can not only make you money but also help build a community that is growing.

Buffalo, New York, isn't just another market; it's a world of untapped possibility where investors' dreams and the needs of the community come together. Every dollar you spend in this city has the potential to make a difference, and it wants you to be a part of its amazing journey. Welcome to Buffalo, a market where every investment tells a story of growth, effect, and success. It's a gem that's easy to miss.

CHAPTER 3
The Benefits for investors under New York State Housing Policies

In this interesting chapter, we look at all the different ways that New York State's forward-thinking housing policies not only make people's lives better but also make money for owners, especially in Buffalo, where things are changing quickly. Because this area is growing so quickly, it shows how state housing programs and business opportunities can work together to help each other.

Housing Opportunities Made Equal (HOME) is a major group in Western New York that works to make sure everyone has access to fair housing. As a civil rights organization, HOME's job is to promote fair housing rules, teach people about them, and make sure they are followed. The goal is to make housing opportunities more equal. The group does great things, like helping people who have been discriminated against in housing, giving free legal advice to landlords and tenants in disagreements, and working to make the housing market more open to everyone. HOME is very important for solving housing problems, making sure that people can find safe, affordable housing, and supporting fairness and equality in the housing sector because it takes a comprehensive approach.

There are many perks for investors. HOME's Security Deposit Assistance and Landlord Training Programs make it easier to handle money and improve property management skills. Programs like the Landlord Reimbursement Program offer financial incentives for property improvements. These programs not only help people follow fair housing rules, but they also make it possible for people to get money back through reimbursement programs.

The part also talks about the work of Investors in Real Estate in Western New York, a non-profit that helps people who want to become real estate investors. This group helps build a group of smart investors by offering learning materials, chances to meet other members, and regular meetings for members. Buffalo Niagara's dedication to promoting and supporting business growth, including in the real estate sector, is also a big plus for the area.

My own experience investing in Section 8 housing in Buffalo is a story of taking chances and getting the most out of the state's policies. Many potential tenants have told me they are looking for affordable living, so my properties have never been short on interest. I often get over one hundred applications for each opening. This steady stream of income and the satisfaction of making a good difference in the community show the double benefit of financial stability and social impact.

Buffalo has a lot of great real estate investment options that are just waiting to be found.

Buffalo's success stories, like the $23.2 million Westminster Commons project, show what can happen when you invest in affordable housing and do it right. The Buffalo Federation of Neighborhood Centers' project, which not only breathes new life into an aging structure but also addresses a pressing need for senior housing and healthcare, demonstrates how such investments can have a significant impact on the neighborhood.

The Governor's holistic housing plan will start a new era for cheap housing in Buffalo and the rest of New York State. This all-encompassing plan focuses on supportive housing, multifamily affordable housing, homeownership possibilities, senior housing, and energy efficiency. It's a goldmine for investors, especially those who want to buy affordable and Section 8 homes.

New York State's housing laws and programs make it easy for real estate investors to make money, especially when it comes to affordable and Section 8 housing. These programs not only offer financial incentives, but they also make the business environment stable and regulated. My experiences and the success of state programs in Buffalo show that investing in this area is a good idea and good for society as a whole. The goal of this chapter is to show why Section 8 investments in Buffalo are a good idea under current state rules and to share what I've learned from working in the field.

Find out in this chapter how New York State's progressive housing policies help residents and make money for investors, especially in Buffalo, which is a place that is growing quickly. New York State, including Buffalo, has a number of housing aid programs that help both residents and investors a great deal:

1. **The HOME Program in New York State:** The goal of this program, which is part of the HOME Investment Partnership Program, is to make more decent, safe, and

affordable housing available in the state. As an example, it helps with buying, fixing up, or building affordable housing, as well as giving low-income people help to buy or rent a house. Housing Opportunities Made Equal (HOME) is a Buffalo, NY-based organization dedicated to promoting the value of fair housing and ensuring equal opportunities for all individuals in the housing market. HOME specializes in advocacy, education, and support to uphold housing rights and combat discrimination. The HOME Program and other state programs make sure that rental projects help families whose incomes are at or below 60% of the area's median income. This is exactly what Section 8 housing standards say must happen.

Benefits for Investors:
- **Security Deposit Assistance:** HOME assists landlords in managing security deposits, streamlining financial transactions with tenants.

- **Landlord Reimbursement Program**: In designated areas, landlords can qualify for a reimbursement of a certain amount they spend on remodeling the property, offering significant financial support for property investments.

- **Landlord Training Programs:** HOME provides educational programs for landlords, covering various aspects of property management and tenant relations. These trainings, conducted by experts, are crucial for investors seeking to enhance their skills and knowledge in effective property management.

By availing of these services and support, investors in Buffalo, particularly those involved in rental properties, can enhance their property management practices, ensure compliance with fair housing laws, and potentially benefit financially through the reimbursement program.

2. **Investors in real estate in western New York**
   - **Focus on Education and Networking:** The goal of this non-profit group is to teach people who are interested in investing in real estate. They provide many learning tools, such as chances to meet other people and hear from experts.

   - **Membership:** Both people and businesses can become members, and there are regular meetings where members can interact and learn.

3. **Invest in the economic growth and support of Buffalo and Niagara:** Buffalo Niagara's main goal is to bring in and help businesses grow in the Buffalo Niagara area, which includes real estate funding.

4. **Range of Services:** They offer a full range of services to businesses and buyers who are looking at the market area. This includes helping to find a site, doing market studies, and running incentive programs.

5. **Comprehensive Support for Diverse Needs**: These programs help people with a lot of different needs, from buying a home to renting an apartment. They do this by providing a helpful environment for both landlords and tenants.

6. **Favorable for Section 8 Investments**: This kind of state-level support makes Section 8 investments in Buffalo more appealing because they make the setting for affordable housing projects more stable and regulated.

A Look at New York State's Programs to Help People Find

Housing

Pay attention to price and quality

Not only do these programs help with regulations, they also give money to make sure that the quality of housing stays good. The money they give covers many costs connected to housing projects, like buying, fixing up, and building

My experience with Section 8 housing in Buffalo, New York, shows the chances and advantages set out by these state rules. Here's a quick summary of what I did:

- **Diverse Tenant Base:** There is a strong desire for affordable housing in Buffalo, and whenever there is a vacancy, my properties get a lot of applications, 100 plus if I quantify.

- **Stable Income Stream:** The Section 8 program's dependable rent payments have given the family a steady income, protecting them from the usual risks that come with investing in real estate.

- **Community Development and Support:** There's more to my interest in Section 8 homes than just making money. It's about making a positive difference in the community by giving people who need it good homes.

People who have done well in Buffalo

Buffalo's $23.2 million Westminster Commons housing and healthcare building for seniors on the city's East Side is a great example of how investments in affordable and supportive housing can pay off. The 84 affordable and supportive apartments in this project show what can happen when well-planned affordable housing investments are made in the city.

The Buffalo Federation of Neighborhood Centers (BFNC) is in charge of the Westminster Commons project. It is a big step forward for senior living and healthcare on Buffalo's East Side.

Important parts of this project are:

- **Senior Housing and Healthcare Project**: This project's main goal is to meet a critical need in the community by building housing and healthcare facilities just for seniors.

- **Renovation of Historic Building:** The Westminster Settlement House, which was built in 1893, will be turned into a community service center as part of the project. This makeover takes into account the building's historical importance while giving it a new purpose for today.

- **Community Involvement**: The project isn't just for the people; it's also for the whole community, which shows how important these kinds of projects are for building and supporting communities.

Investment by the State in Buffalo

More than 3,200 affordable homes have been built or saved in Buffalo thanks to more than $307 million in investments made by New York State Homes and Community Renewal since 2011. With this big investment, the state shows its dedication to affordable homes and the chances it offers for investors

A Complete Plan for Housing

In 2023, Kathy Hochul, the governor of New York State, announced a historic $25 billion housing plan that would build and maintain 100,000 affordable homes across the state, including in Buffalo. Real estate investors who focus on affordable homes and Section 8 properties will benefit the most from this plan. Data Source

Important parts of the plan

The plan has several parts that will directly help investors:

- **Creation and Preservation of Supportive Housing:** $1.5 billion is set aside for supportive housing, which meets the needs of people and families who need supportive services and is similar to the Section 8 housing plan.

- **Multifamily Affordable Housing:** $1 billion is set aside to build new multifamily affordable housing, which means that owners have a lot of chances to get involved in new development projects.

- **Homeownership Opportunities:** $400 million is set aside to improve homeownership opportunities, especially in places that aren't well served. This can be a big draw for investors interested in low-income family housing.

- **Senior Housing:** An investment of $300 million in senior housing meets the growing need for places to live that are good for older people and creates another way to invest in real estate.

- **Electrification and Energy Efficiency**: The plan includes $250 million to make low-income housing units more energy efficient. This will allow owners to improve their properties while also helping with sustainability efforts.

Additional Measures of Support

The state budget also takes care of other living issues:

- **Conversion of Vacant Properties:** The Housing Our Neighbors With Dignity Act has been given $100 million to make it easier to turn empty business properties into homes. This is a one-of-a-kind investment opportunity.

- **Funding for Accessory Dwelling Units:** $85 million is given to bring accessory dwelling units, such as basement flats and garage units, up to code. This makes it easier to build homes and invest in real estate.

- **Land Banks and Redevelopment:** $50 million has been set aside for land banks to buy and rebuild empty or abandoned homes. This can help investors who want to bring houses back to life.

- **Rural and Neighborhood Preservation Programs:** For the first time in more than 40 years, these programs have gotten more money, totaling more than $18 million. This funding will take care of local housing needs in all communities and neighborhoods across the state. This is very important for investors who are interested in rural and community-based real estate projects. Data Source

Final Thoughts

As we come to the end of this insightful chapter on the benefits for investors under New York State Housing Policies, it's clear that real estate investment is a great time, especially in Buffalo. The idea that state policies and investor success work hand-in-hand is not just a theory; the healthy community and strong market growth are proof of this. Initiatives like the HOME Program and Governor Kathy Hochul's complete housing plan are more than just rules; they are forces for good that make things better and provide a stable and profitable environment for investors, especially in Section 8 and affordable housing.

The story of my time living in Section 8 housing in Buffalo shows how these laws can work and provide benefits. There is a lot of interest in cheap housing; it brings in steady income, and it has a big effect on the community. My experience shows that being financially stable and socially responsible are both very good things. The success stories, like the Westminster Commons project, show how well-planned investments in the community can change things for the better.

As we close this chapter, let it be a lighthouse for investors, both those who are already investing and those who want to start. New York, and especially Buffalo, is more than just a place to invest. It's a world of opportunities where financial goals and community growth can come together. The state has always been committed to affordable homes, which opens up a lot of possibilities. It doesn't matter if you're an experienced investor or just starting out. The message is clear: Buffalo is a land of potential, and now is the time to explore, invest, and do well. This chapter will show you how to invest in real estate in a city that is growing and is also accepting investors with open arms to be a part of its amazing journey.

The complete housing plan and supporting measures in New York State make it easy for real estate investors, especially those who want to buy affordable or Section 8 housing, to make smart decisions. These programs not only offer cash incentives, but they also make the environment for investments more stable and long-lasting. These programs can help investors in Buffalo, NY, and other parts of the state build, improve, and manage homes that meet the growing need for affordable housing and assist in the growth of the city. Buffalo, NY, is a great place to invest in Section 8 properties because the state's policies are friendly, the real estate market is strong, and people have made good money by investing there. My journey and the state's programs show that investing in this area is a good idea and has a positive effect on society. This chapter's goal is to make it clear how state policies make Section 8 investments in Buffalo more appealing and to share what I've learned from working in the field.

CHAPTER 4
My Real Estate Journey - Insights and Calculations in Great Detail

When you invest in real estate, the process is just as important as the end goal. Making plans ahead of time, doing a lot of studying, and being dedicated to quality have helped me get where I am in this ever-changing field, especially when it comes to Section 8 housing in Buffalo, NY. This chapter goes into great detail about my investment strategy, the math I use to make choices, and the lessons I've learned from each property I've bought. It's a journey with smart changes, calculated risks, and a deep knowledge of how the Buffalo market works.

At the heart of my investment approach is a basic idea: quality comes first. This philosophy is clear from the fact that all of my homes have had major repairs and improvements made to them. I've made sure that every property not only meets but also exceeds market standards by focusing on high-quality materials and modern features. This dedication to excellence has been very helpful in finding dependable tenants, making the properties last longer and be worth more, and ultimately making my investments profitable.

Before you rent the house to someone else, you should think about whether you would let your own child live there.

It's important where you live in real estate. When I choose properties in Buffalo, I base my decisions on a lot of study and analysis. I look into demographic trends, growth prospects, and neighborhood traits using tools such as Niche and NeighborhoodScout. Using this data-driven method helps me find places that are likely to go up in value and have a lot of tenants. By putting my money into properties in well-thought-out areas, I make sure that each one is not only a benefit for now but also a good investment for the future.

If you read this chapter, I'll show you all of my Buffalo properties in great depth. Each property has a unique tale to tell, supported by data and wise decisions. They range from a duplex in Lovejoy to a modern retreat in Kaisertown. You'll see how great returns on investment (ROI) can come from both high-quality improvements and smart location choices. For people who want to become investors, these case studies show how the rules of successful real estate investing work in real life.

My investment strategy is based on putting quality first. This way of thinking is clear from the big repairs and improvements that were made to each home. By putting a focus on high-quality materials and modern amenities, I made sure that every property not only met but also exceeded what the market anticipated. This dedication to quality not only brings in reliable renters, but it also helps the properties last longer and be worth more.

Analyzing Areas for Potential

When investing in real estate, picking the right spot is very important, especially in a market as diverse as Buffalo, NY. Each property is picked after a lot of study, using tools like **Niche** and **NeighborhoodScout** to look at things like demographic trends, growth potential, and the characteristics of the neighborhood. These tools give you information about the local economy, the rental market, and the demand from tenants, all of which are important for making smart choices. By putting my money into areas where prices are likely to go up and where people want to rent, I make sure that each property is not only an advantage now but also an investment that will pay off in the future. This smart choice of place is in line with knowing how markets work and what economic indicators show, which are important for making money in real estate investing.

Along with these tools, I also think about things like plans for future growth in the area, different ways to pay for things, and the legal and tax effects of having and renting out properties. This all-around method makes sure that every investment I make is safe, profitable, and in line with my investment strategy's long-term goals.

Emphasizing Quality and Strategic Location Selection

- **Location, location, and location:** Choosing properties in locations with potential for growth in Buffalo, NY, is crucial. Resources like **Zillow** or **Realtor.com** provide valuable insights into neighborhood characteristics, property values, and trends, helping to identify areas that are desirable for Section 8 tenants.

- **Market Trends:** Understanding market trends is key. Websites like **Trulia** offer data on local real estate trends, rental market conditions, and historical property values in Buffalo, aiding in making informed investment decisions.

- **Property Value Appreciation Potential:** To assess the

potential for property value appreciation, tools like **Redfin** provide market reports and forecasts. This helps in selecting properties in neighborhoods with promising growth trajectories.

- **Rental Yield:** Calculating the potential rental yield is essential. Online calculators on websites like **Investopedia** can help estimate the return on investment based on rental income and property costs.

- **Property Condition:** Evaluating the condition of each property is vital. Online resources like **HomeAdvisor** can be used to estimate repair and renovation costs, ensuring that the property meets and exceeds Section 8 standards.

- **Local Real Estate Market:** Understanding the local real estate market in Buffalo is crucial. **City-Data** provides demographic and real estate data, helping to gauge the market's health and potential.

- **Economic Indicators:** Analyzing economic indicators in Buffalo is important. Websites like the **Bureau of Economic Analysis** offer insights into local economic trends, employment rates, and economic growth, which can impact the real estate market.

- **Property Management Costs:** Estimating property management costs is essential. Online resources like **All Property Management** can provide estimates and information on property management services in Buffalo.

- **Legal and Tax Implications:** Understanding the legal and tax implications is crucial. Websites like **NOLO** offer guidance on landlord-tenant laws and property taxes in New York.

- **Financing Options:** Exploring financing options is key. Websites like **Bankrate** provide information on mortgage rates, loan options, and financial calculators.

- **Tenant Demand:** Assessing tenant demand in Buffalo is important. Rentometer can be used to analyze rental market demand and average rent prices in specific neighborhoods.

- **Future Development Plans in the Area:** Keeping informed about future development plans in Buffalo can impact investment decisions. Local government websites and planning portals, like **Buffalo's Official Website**, often provide information on upcoming infrastructure and development projects.

- **Insurance Costs:** Understanding insurance costs is necessary. Websites like **Insurance.com** offer quotes and information on property insurance rates in New York.

- **Maintenance and Repair Costs:** Estimating maintenance and repair costs is crucial for budgeting. Online tools like **HomeWyse** provide cost estimates for home repairs and maintenance in specific locations.

- **Exit Strategy Options:** Considering exit strategy options for each investment is wise. Real estate websites like **BiggerPockets** offer resources and forums discussing various exit strategies in real estate investing.

Each of these points, along with the suggested online resources, can provide a comprehensive approach to investing in Section 8 properties in Buffalo, NY, ensuring that every aspect of the investment is well-researched and informed.

My Journey with Section 8

Quality is the most important thing to me when it comes to investing. This way of thinking is clear from the significant repairs and improvements that were made to each property. I made sure that each property not only met market standards but also far exceeded them by putting a lot of emphasis on using high-quality materials and up-to-date facilities. This kind of dedication to quality is important for getting reliable renters and making the properties last longer and be worth more. Let me share with you some information about my investment properties:

Property # 1: The duplex in Lovejoy, Buffalo

This duplex, which has around 1,550 square feet of room inside, is my first purchase in Buffalo's real estate market. The house was updated with new PEX wiring and glass block windows after it was bought for $100,000 and fixed up for $25,000. Inside, there are tile, vinyl, and other types of floors, as well as a gas water heater. It looks better from the street because it has composite walls and an asphalt roof.

- **Place and Market Appeal:** The house is in an easy-to-get-to part of Buffalo, which makes it appealing to renters who value convenience. Because it's a duplex, there are different ways to rent it, which makes it a good choice in a busy area.

- **The money side and return on investment (ROI):** The total amount of money put into this building is $125,000. With a $2,000 monthly rental income, the yearly rental income is $24,000. By dividing the annual rental income by the total investment, one can calculate the ROI, which is about 19.2%. This is a great return in a strong real estate market.

Property # 2: A single-family home in Lovejoy, Buffalo

This single-family home has 3 bedrooms, 1 bathroom, and was bought for $70,000 plus an extra $15,000. It is around 1,250 square feet and has been improved. On the main level, there is an eat-in kitchen and a bedroom. The floors are hardwood, tile, and vinyl.

- **Place and Market Appeal:** The house is in Lovejoy, Buffalo, which has a Walk Score of 58, which means it's somewhat walkable. A concrete and dirt path makes up for the lack of a garage, and the 4,050-square-foot lot size gives you plenty of space outside.

- **The money side and return on investment (ROI):** This property was bought for $85,000, and it rents for $1,300 a month, for a total of $15,600 a year. In the Buffalo market, this means that the ROI is about 18.4%, which is a good return.

Property # 3: A modern retreat in Kaisertown, Buffalo

As stated in the introduction, this single-family home has a mix of modern and classic styles. The four-bedroom, 1.5-bathroom house cost a total of $102,000 to buy and fix up.

- **Renovation and Appeal:** The house has a new roof, siding, and windows, among other changes. Both the kitchen and baths were updated in a stylish way, and the backyard is a nice place to relax.

- **The money side and return on investment (ROI):** The rental income from the house is $1,500 per month, or $18,000 per year. This results in a ROI of about 17.6%, demonstrating how much value thoughtful renovations and new updates add.

Property # 3: The Triplex Project in Kaisertown, Buffalo

This triplex was built in the late 1800s, has 3 apartments, and is around 2,000 square feet. It was bought for $80,000. The improvement cost was $50,000, which shows how it could be used as a multifamily home.

- **Place and Market Appeal:** The property needs some work, but it has a lot of potential to add a lot of value. It's in the Kaisertown neighborhood, close to schools and other services, so it's a good choice for a wide range of potential tenants.

- **The money side and return on investment (ROI):** The total amount that will be spent is $130,000. With a total rental income of $3,000 plus per month, the yearly income is $36,000, with an expected return on investment (ROI) of about 27.7%.

Final Thoughts

In order to sum up how I invest in real estate, especially Section 8 housing, I need to stress the two things that have made me successful: a strong dedication to quality and a smart focus on location. Do not think of these principles as vague ideas; they are real methods that have worked well in the Buffalo, NY, real estate market over and over again.

The focus on quality isn't just a selling point; it's one of the most important things to me when I spend. I make sure that every property in my stock stands out in the market by fixing it up and making big improvements. Using high-quality materials and adding modern features that today's renters want are part of this method. This kind of dedication to quality does more than just bring in reliable renters; it also makes each property last longer and be worth more on the market. Long-term, this means steady rental income and a strong rise in property value, both of which are important signs of a good investment.

Choosing the right location is very important, especially when it comes to Section 8 housing. I didn't pick different places in Buffalo, NY, by chance; I did it because I knew a lot about the area's real estate market, changes in population, and the needs of Section 8 tenants. The right location can have a big effect on a number of important factors, including the stability of tenants, the demand for rentals, and the general safety of an investment. It's because of these factors that I've been able to make sure that each property not only meets the wants of the community but also makes a good investment.

This in-depth look at my experience with four homes in Buffalo, NY, shows how to invest wisely in real estate. As a result of its own unique story of quality improvements and smart location choices, each building adds to a bigger story of success. The excellent return on investments (ROIs) show that this method works. Aspiring real estate owners can learn from these case studies, which show how focusing on both quality and location can lead to profitable and long-lasting investments.

To sum up, my investment approach, which is based on quality and location, works especially well for Section 8 housing. This strategy has not only made money for the company, but it has also helped make apartments that people want to live in. It's an example of how Section 8 investments can pay off if they are made with care, foresight, and a dedication to quality. People who want to become investors can learn a lot from this method and use it in their real estate deals, especially in markets like Buffalo, NY. This mix of quality and smart location choice is, in fact, the key to long-term, profitable real estate investment in the Section 8 field.

CHAPTER 5
Passing the inspection of Section 8 The big mountain to cross

The purpose of this chapter is to give a thorough outline of the requirements and standards needed for Section 8 housing inspections. It does this by using a variety of sources, such as HUD guidelines and the knowledge of seasoned real estate pros. Now I will go over the details of the HUD guidelines for inspecting a Section 8 property. You can download the checklist from the HUD website.

In Buffalo, NY, Section 8 housing inspections are like climbing a difficult mountain: they are very complicated and hard to understand. People who are interested in investing can use this chapter as a complete guide to help them pass these tests. Not only is it about checking things off a list, but it is also about knowing the complex rules and regulations that govern Section 8 housing and making sure that properties are not only legal but also safe and comfortable for tenants.

If you want to know how to go through the inspection process, this chapter goes into great depth about the HUD rules and uses the knowledge of seasoned real estate professionals. The first step is to fully understand the general inspection criteria, which include things like unit types, addresses, and information about the owner. Each of these plays a very important role in the result of the inspection.

Then we talk about the specific review rules for different parts of a house, like kitchens, bathrooms, living rooms, and more. These insights are very important for investors to find weak spots, make plans for repair, and follow the rules.

> *Before the official Section 8 review, you should do your own inspection to make sure you're happy with your property.*

This part also covers more than just the basics of passing inspections. It stresses that investors are responsible for building houses that are safe, healthy, and community-minded. You're not just making a business investment when you put money into Section 8 housing; you're also making society better by giving families good homes and keeping neighborhoods strong.

As you start or continue your journey as an owner in Section 8 housing, keep in mind that the choices and actions you take will have a big effect. This chapter is meant to give you the information and ideas you need to not only pass inspections but also make a real change in the lives of your tenants and the community as a whole. If you want to invest in Section 8 housing, you're in for a ride full of rules, care, and building communities.

General Information: Inspection of a Section 8 home
The "General Information" part of a Section 8 housing inspection is the most important part because it sets the stage for the rest of the exam. This part covers a number of important points:

- **Unit Type:** This tells you what kind of living unit it is. This can include types of homes like single-family homes, flats, townhouses, duplexes, and mobile homes. Some inspection factors may be different for each type of unit because each type of housing may have its own set of rules or standards.

- **Unit Address:** This is the unit's actual address, which includes the city, state, and zip code. The location is very important because it may decide which local rules or codes apply in addition to the federal Section 8 standards. Because of local rules or the environment, some places may have extra requirements.

- **Owner Information:** Information about the person who owns the land or the company that takes care of it. This usually includes the name, contact information, and maybe some other information, like what kind of relationship the owner has with the renter (if any). This information is necessary for communication and any steps that need to be taken after the inspection.

- **Type of Inspection:** Section 8 allows for different types of checks, such as;

  o   Before a renter moves in, the unit must pass the initial inspection to make sure it meets HUD's Housing Quality Standards (HQS).

  o   Annual Inspection: Regular checks to make sure that HQS rules are still being followed.

  o   Complaint Inspection: This type of inspection is based on a specific complaint or request and looks into issues or concerns made by tenants or other people.

  o   Quality Control Inspection: The Public Housing Authority (PHA) does random checks to make sure that inspectors and landlords follow HQS.

  o   An emergency inspection is done when there is a direct threat to the health or safety of the tenant.

It's important to understand general knowledge for a number of reasons, including:

- **Compliance:** Makes sure that the unit is being inspected according to the right rules and standards, which can be different depending on the type of unit and where it is located.

- **Keeping Records:** Both landlords and housing officials need to keep accurate records so they can be held accountable and look them up later.

- **Communication**: The owner's information is needed for any follow-up that needs to be done, like repairs, extra paperwork, or dealing with any compliance problems.

- **Understanding the Situation:** This kind of inspection gives both the tester and the landlord information about the situation. For instance, the first inspection might cover more ground, while the yearly inspection might focus on what's changed since the last check.

Living Room: Section 8 Housing Inspection Requirements
Section 8 reviews have certain rules about the living room, which is usually in the middle of a house. These rules make sure that the place is safe, habitable, and comfortable for the people who live there. The most important things checked in the living room are:

- **Presence:** A living room is an essential part of life. It should be a separate place that is meant to be used every day.

- **Electricity:** There must be at least two working electricity outlets in the living room, or one outlet and one permanent light fixture. This makes sure that there is enough power for lights and other electronics.

- **No hazards in the room:** It should be free of anything that could be harmful to health or safety. Some things that count as tripping risks are exposed wiring, big cracks or holes in the walls or ceilings, and so on.

- **Security:** The windows and doors in the living room must be locked and secured to keep everyone inside safe. This includes making sure that locks and doors work properly.

- **Window Conditions:** Every living room must have at least one window that can be opened and has locks that work. For good insulation and safety, windows should not have any cracks or holes in them.

- **Conditions of the ceiling:** The ceiling must be in good shape, with no major damage like big holes or cracks. There shouldn't be any leaks or water harm.

- **Wall Conditions:** Walls should be steady and whole, with no major damage like big holes or cracks. If you don't want to be exposed to lead-based paint, you should fix any peeling paint, especially in older buildings. Long story short: paint the house well before listing.

- **Conditions of the Floor:** The floors must be solid and not sagging. They also can't have any dangerous flaws like big holes or weak floorboards. It should be safe to walk on the top without getting hurt. Imagine if you would allow your kids to live here!

- **Lead-Based Paint:** The paint shouldn't be breaking, peeling, or cracking. This could mean that the paint has lead-based paint, which is very bad for your health.

- **Smoke alarms:** Smoke alarms are an important safety feature. Local codes say that they need to be put in in certain places, like each bedroom and the halls next to them. Detectors need to work and should be checked often.

Each of these parts is important for the reasons below:

- **Safety and Health:** Making sure the building is safe electrically, structurally, and free of dangers is good for the people who live or work there.

- **Comfort and Livability:** The living room is a good place to do everyday things because it has enough light, safe windows, and well-kept surfaces.

- **Standards Compliance:** Meeting these requirements makes sure that the property meets HUD's Housing Quality Standards, which are needed for Section 8 funds to be valid.

The Inspection Method
Each part is carefully looked at during the check. A checklist is often used by inspectors to make sure that everything is looked at. Some of the things they might check are the electrical outlets, the window and door locks, the walls, ceilings, and floors for damage, and any signs of lead-based paint dangers, especially in older homes.

Recording and fixing the problem
Any problems that were found during the check need to be written down in the inspector's report. The owner of the building is then responsible for fixing things or making them better. Sometimes, there may need to be a second check to make sure that all problems have been properly fixed. Section 8 reviews have strict rules about the living room because it is the heart of the house. These rules are meant to make sure that the area is safe, useful, and comfortable for the people who live or work there. Property owners should take care of these areas themselves to make sure they are in compliance and give their renters a good place to live.

Standards for Kitchens: Section 8 Home Inspection
When it comes to Section 8 inspections, the kitchen is one of

the most important rooms in any house. It has to meet certain standards to make sure it is safe, useful, and good for both preparing and storing food. The kitchen check looks at a few important things:

- **Area Presence:** There must be a separate kitchen area. It should be made clear that it is for cooking and preparing food. Unlike that, there is a stove next to the living room area, and we call it the kitchen.

- **Electrical Standards:** The kitchen must have at least two outlets that work or one outlet and one fixed light fixture. This makes sure that there is enough power for the lights and appliances in the kitchen.

- **Safety:** The kitchen needs to be safe, just like the rest of the house. This includes making sure that the locks on the windows and doors work to keep the people inside safe.

- **Window Conditions:** If there are windows in the kitchen, they should be able to be opened and closed, not cracked, and have locks that work. This is important for both protection and air flow.

- **Conditions of the ceiling:** The ceiling must be in good shape, with no major flaws like big holes, cracks, or signs of water damage or leaks.

- **Wall Conditions:** Walls should be steady and not have any big holes, cracks, or paint that is peeling off. This is especially important in older buildings where lead-based paint could be present.

- **Floor Conditions:** The floor must be solid and safe, with no big holes, loose floorboards, or other noticeable wear that could make it easy to trip.

- **Stove and Oven:** The kitchen needs to have a stove and oven that work. They should be in good shape and have all the buttons, burners, and, if necessary, oven heating elements that work properly. It is the responsibility of the owner to arrange them.

- **Refrigerator:** There must be a working refrigerator that is the right size for the unit. It should stay in a setting that is safe for storing food. The U.S. Department of Housing and Urban Development (HUD) has rules about appliances, like freezers, that can be used in Section 8 housing. HUD has detailed rules about how these appliances should work and be safe, but the exact size of the fridge needed can change based on the unit size and the number of people living there.

  - **Size Requirements:**
    - **Size:** The fridge should be the right size for the room. This means it should be big enough to hold enough food for everyone living in the house. One example is that a larger family would need a bigger fridge than a single person.

    - **Effective Design:** The fridge needs to be in good shape and keep a steady temperature that is safe for keeping food. Usually, this means keeping the temperature below 40°F (4°C) so that food doesn't go bad and bad germs don't grow.

    - **Energy Efficiency:** This isn't a straight requirement for size, but it is something that is often thought about. Models that use less energy are better because they help lower power costs and are better for the environment.

- **Sink:** The kitchen must have a sink that works and is linked to a sewage system so that hot and cold water can run through it. There shouldn't be any big leaks in the sink, and it should drain well. Also, the water should drain properly from the sink.

- **Food Storage Room:** You need to have enough room to store food. This can include shelves or drawers that are clean, safe, and useful. The cabinets should be in good working condition.

- **Lead-Based Paint:** Paint that is chipping, peeling, or cracking shouldn't be present in buildings. This could be a sign of lead-based paint.

These rules are very important because these things:

- **Health and Safety:** Making sure that kitchen tools work and are safe, as well as the building's structural integrity, is very important for everyone's health and safety.

- **Hygiene and Food Safety:** Having the right places to store and prepare food is important for keeping things clean and avoiding getting sick from food.

- **Compliance with Standards:** The property must meet these requirements in order to be eligible for Section 8 funds because they are in line with HUD's Housing Quality Standards.

The Inspection Method

During the check, every part of the kitchen is looked at carefully. Inspectors use a thorough list to make sure that everything meets the standards. They usually check the electrical outlets, make sure the machines work, make sure the windows and doors are locked, and look at the kitchen as a whole. Any problems found during the check need to be written down. The owner of the property is responsible for fixing these problems, which could mean fixing or replacing equipment, fixing problems with the structure, or getting rid of any lead-based paint hazards. It's common to need to do another check to make sure that all the changes have been made.

The kitchen is one of the most important parts of Section 8 housing checks. There are rules in place to make sure it is safe, useful, and clean. To make sure their kitchens meet these standards, property owners should keep them in good shape on a daily basis. This will provide tenants with a good place to live and meet Section 8 requirements.

Bathroom Requirements: Section 8 Home Inspection
In Section 8 housing inspections, the bathroom is a very important room that must meet certain standards to be safe, useful, and clean. The bathroom check looks at a few important things:

- **Placement:** The apartment has to have at least one bathroom. For personal hygiene, it should be a different, private area.

- **Toilet:** The bathroom must have a toilet that works and has a seat that is stable and safe. It should work right to flush and not leak.

- **Washbasin:** You need a washbasin that works and has both hot and cold water going through it. To work properly, it should be hooked up to a sewage system, have no big leaks, and drain water away.

- **Shower or tub:** The unit must have a shower or tub that works and has hot and cold running water. That means it should be in good shape, not leak, and drain well.

- **Electrical Standards:** The bathroom should have a light bulb or at least one electrical outlet that works. This makes sure there is enough light and that the electricity is safe.

- **Security:** If the bathroom has windows, they should be locked and safe. This is important for the people living there to protect their privacy and safety.

- **Window Conditions:** All windows should be able to be opened for air flow, not have any cracks, and have locks that work. Bathrooms need to have good airflow to keep moisture from building up and mold from growing.

- **Conditions of the ceiling:** The ceiling must be in good shape, with no major flaws like big holes, cracks, or signs of water damage or leaks.

- **Conditions of the Walls:** The walls should be steady and not have any big holes, cracks, or paint that is coming off. Lead-based paint is dangerous and needs to be taken care of in older houses.

- **Floor Conditions:** The floor must be solid and not sagging. It also can't have any big holes or loose beams that could be dangerous. To keep things clean, it should also be waterproof and easy to clean.

- **Air Flow:** To keep moisture and mold from growing, you need enough air. This can happen through an open window or an air fan that works.

- **Lead-Based Paint:** Paint that is chipping, peeling, or cracking shouldn't be present in buildings. This could be a sign of lead-based paint.

These rules are very important because these things:

- **Health and Hygiene:** Making sure that bathroom features work and are clean is important for people's health and hygiene.

- **Safety:** Electrical safety, structural stability, and windows and doors that lock are all important for the people living there.

- **Compliance with Standards:** The property must meet these requirements in order to be eligible for Section 8 funds because they are in line with HUD's Housing Quality Standards.

During the check, every part of the bathroom is looked at carefully. Inspectors use a thorough list to make sure that everything meets the standards. Usually, they check the electrical outlets, the plumbing fixtures to make sure they work, the windows and doors to make sure they are locked, and the general condition of the bathroom. Any problems found during the check need to be written down. The owner of the property is responsible for fixing these problems, which could mean fixing or replacing fixtures, fixing problems with the structure, or getting rid of any lead-based paint dangers. It's common to need to do another check to make sure that all the changes have been made.

Section 8 Housing Inspection of Other Living Areas and Halls
Section 8 housing checks look at more than just the main living room, kitchen, and bathroom. They also look at other living rooms and hallways. These places are very important for the safety and functionality of the whole house. The check looks at a few important things:

- **Room Codes:** Every room must follow the city building and occupancy rules. This includes the right size, ways to get out, and suitability for the purpose (for example, beds, dining rooms).

- **Electricity:** All living rooms and hallways should have enough electrical outlets or fixed light fixtures that work. This makes sure that people have enough lighting and electricity.

- **Risks:** These places must not have any risks to health or safety. This includes, but isn't limited to, wire that is visible, big holes or cracks in the walls or ceilings, and anything that could cause someone to trip.

- **Safety:** The doors and windows in these places must be safe and able to be locked. This is very important for the people living there to keep them safe and private.

- **Window Conditions:** Windows should be able to be opened and closed, have no cracks, and have locks that work. This is necessary for safety, air flow, and natural light.

- **Conditions of the ceiling:** The ceilings must be in good shape, with no major damage like big holes, cracks, or signs of water damage or leaks.

- **Conditions of the Walls:** The walls should be steady and not have any big holes, cracks, or paint that is coming off. Lead-based paint is dangerous and needs to be taken care of in older houses.

- **Conditions of the Floor:** The floors must be solid and not sagging. They also can't have any dangerous flaws like big holes or weak floorboards. You should be able to walk on them without getting hurt.

- **Smoke alarms:** Smoke alarms are an important safety feature. Local codes say that they need to be put in certain places, like each bedroom and the halls next to them. Detectors need to work and should be checked often.

These rules are very important because these things:

- **Safety and Health:** Making sure the building is safe electrically, structurally, and free of dangers is good for the people who live or work there.

- **Fire Safety:** Smoke monitors that work properly are necessary to let you know about a fire quickly, which makes things a lot safer.

- **Standards Compliance:** Meeting these requirements makes sure that the property meets HUD's Housing Quality Standards, which are needed for Section 8 funds to be valid.

During the inspection, every part of the other living rooms and halls is carefully looked at. A checklist is often used by inspectors to make sure that everything is looked at. As part of their job, they might check the electrical outlets, the locks on the windows and doors, the walls, the ceilings, and the floors for damage, and the smoke alarms' placement and functionality. Any problems that were found during the check need to be written down in the inspector's report. The owner of the building is then responsible for fixing things or making them better. Sometimes, there may need to be a second check to make sure that all problems have been properly fixed. Other living rooms and hallways are important parts of a house that need to meet certain standards for Section 8 inspections. These rules are meant to make sure that the places are safe, useful, and comfortable for the people who live or work there. Property owners should take care of these areas themselves to make sure they are in compliance and give their renters a good place to live.

Section 8 Housing Inspection of Secondary Rooms and the Outside of the Building

Section 8 housing checks cover more than just the main living areas. They also look at secondary rooms and the outside of the building. These places are very important for the property's safety, structural integrity, and ability to be lived in. The check looks at a few important things:

- **Security:** Extra rooms like basements, attics, and storage areas should be safe. This includes making sure that the locks on the windows and doors work to keep the people inside safe.

- **Risks:** These places must not have any health or safety risks. This includes wiring that is uncovered, major structure damage, and any other problem that could put people inside at risk.

- **Base:** The building's base must be stable and whole, with no major cracks or damage that could weaken the structure of the building.

- **Decks, stairs, and porches:** Decks, stairs, and porches must be safe and in good shape. This includes steps that are safe and don't have any major cracks or other dangers, as well as railings that are secure on stairs and porches.

- **Roof and Gutters:** The roof and gutter system should be in good shape to make sure water drains properly and doesn't get inside. No shingles should be missing, there should be no major damage, and the drains should not be clogged.

- **Exterior Surfaces:** The walls, windows, and doors on the outside should be in good shape and not have any major damage or wear and tear. This includes keeping the paint, walls, and other surfaces in good shape.

- **Chimney:** If the house has a chimney, it should be stable and in good shape. This means there are no broken bricks or blocks and the lid is on right to keep water out.

- **Lead-Based Paint:** The paint shouldn't be breaking, peeling, or cracking. This could mean that the paint has lead-based paint, which is very bad for your health.

These rules are very important because these things:

- **Safety and security:** Making sure that extra rooms and the outside of the building are safe and secure is important for everyone's health.

- **Structural Integrity:** The base, roof, and outside surfaces must be kept in good shape for the property to last and be livable in the future.

- **Compliance with Standards:** The property must meet these requirements in order to be eligible for Section 8 funds because they are in line with HUD's Housing Quality Standards.

The Inspection Method

During the check, every part of the secondary rooms and the outside of the building is carefully looked at. Inspectors use a thorough list to make sure that everything meets the standards. Most of the time, they check the base, stairs, railings, roof, gutters, exterior surfaces, and chimneys. Any problems found during the check need to be written down. The owner of the property is responsible for fixing these problems, which could mean making repairs or changes to make the property safer and more in line with HUD standards. It's common to need to do another check to make sure that all the changes have been made. Part 8 housing checks pay a lot of attention to secondary rooms and the outside of the building. There are certain rules that these places must follow to make sure they are safe, secure, and help keep the property's structure strong. Proprietors must keep these areas in good shape and pay attention to them on a regular basis to meet Section 8 standards and give tenants a good place to live.

Plumbing and heating: Section 8 home inspection

Heating and plumbing are important parts of Section 8 housing checks, with the main goal of making sure that heating systems are safe and working properly. These things are very important for the people living there's happiness, health, and safety. Several important places are checked out:

- **Adequacy and Safety of Heating Equipment:** - The home must have a heating system that is safe and works.
    - The weather should be able to stay healthy and comfortable.
    - There can't be any dangers in the system, like gas leaks, bad venting, or electrical links that aren't safe.

- **Airflow/Cooling:** Enough airflow is needed to keep the air clean and stop moisture from building up. If there is air conditioning, it should be in good working order, but it's not necessary.

- **Water Heater:** The house must have a water heater that is properly installed and works.
    - It should have enough hot water for everyone in the house and be set to a safe temperature, usually around 120°F to avoid burning.
    - The water heater should have the right airflow and not be a safety risk in any way.

- **Water Supply:** The house must have a proper and constant water supply. The water should be clean enough to meet state health standards.
    - All water fixtures, like sinks, toilets, bathtubs, and showers, must be in good shape.
    - All of the taps should have hot and cold running water, and there shouldn't be any leaks.
    - Drains must work properly and not get clogged up too much.

- **Sewer Connection:** The land must be hooked up to a septic or sanitary sewer system that is in good shape. The drain shouldn't back up or leak.

These rules are very important because these things:

- **Health and Comfort:** Proper plumbing and heating are necessary for the people living there to be healthy and comfortable.

- **Safety:** Making sure that heating systems and water heaters are safe is very important to keep crashes and other problems from happening.

- **Sanitation:** Making sure the water works is important for keeping the house clean.

- **Compliance with Standards:** The property must meet these requirements in order to be eligible for Section 8 funds because they are in line with HUD's Housing Quality Standards.

The Inspection Method

Every part of the plumbing and heating systems is carefully looked at during the check. Inspectors use a thorough list to make sure that everything meets the standards. For example, they check all plumbing fixtures, heaters, water heaters, and the water source to make sure everything works and is safe. Any problems that were found during the check need to be written down in the inspector's report. The owner of the building is then responsible for fixing things or making them better. Sometimes, there may need to be a second check to make sure that all problems have been properly fixed. Heating and plumbing are two of the most important parts of Section 8 home inspections. These systems have to meet certain requirements to make sure they are safe, work properly, and add to the property's habitability as a whole. Property owners must keep these systems in good shape and pay attention to them on a regular basis to meet Section 8 standards and give their tenants a good place to live.

General Health and Safety: Section 8 housing inspection
When Section 8 housing inspectors look at a home, they focus on making sure it is safe and healthy for everyone living there. This thorough check looks at many things, including:

- **Access:** It must be safe and easy to get to the place. The entrances and exits should be clear of any dangers or obstacles.

- **Fire Exits:** There must be enough fire exits that are not blocked. Fire exits must follow the rules for fire safety in your area.

- **Infestation Evidence:** - There should be no signs of rodents, bugs, or other pests living on the land. To keep this standard, regular pest control methods should be used.

- **Garbage/Debris:** - The land should not have a lot of trash and other junk on it. - This is important for keeping it clean and avoiding pest problems.

- **Refuse Disposal:** - There must be enough places to get rid of trash. This includes proper trash cans or a set place for trash.

- **Interior Stairs and Halls:** The stairs and halls inside the building should be safe and well-kept. This includes safe fences, enough lighting, and paths that aren't blocked.

- **Other Dangers:** - There shouldn't be any other health and safety risks on the land. This includes wires that are bare, fittings that aren't tight, and dangerous materials.

- **Elevators:** If the building has elevators, they need to be in good shape and up to safety standards. Maintenance and checks must be done on a regular basis.

- **Air Quality:** - People who live or work in a building need good air quality for their health. This means having enough air flow and no harmful gasses or pollutants.

- **Conditions of the Site and Neighborhood:** The general condition of the site and neighborhood is looked at. This covers things like how safe, clean, and noisy the place is.

- **Lead-Based Paint Certification:** – Buildings built before 1978 may need to have a lead-based paint check. Homeowners may have to show proof that their homes don't have any lead-based paint dangers.

These rules are very important because these things:

- **Safety and Health:** Making sure that people live in a safe and healthy setting is very important for their health.

- **Fire Safety:** There must be enough fire exits and safety steps in case of an emergency.

- **Pest Control:** Keeping bugs away is good for your health and comfort.

- Good air quality and proper trash removal are important for an environmentally healthy living space.

- **Compliance with Standards:** The property must meet these requirements in order to be eligible for Section 8 funds because they are in line with HUD's Housing Quality Standards.

The Inspection Method

Every aspect of general health and safety is carefully looked at during the review. Inspectors use a thorough list to make sure that everything meets the standards. Usually, they check the property's access points, fire safety measures, signs of infestation, trash disposal facilities, and general state. Any problems that were found during the check need to be written down in the inspector's report. The owner of the building is then responsible for fixing things or making them better. Sometimes, there may need to be a second check to make sure that all problems have been properly fixed. Health and safety in general are very important during Section 8 housing checks. These rules are meant to make sure that renters live in a safe, healthy, and comfortable place. Property owners should take care of their homes so that they meet these standards. This will make sure that they follow Section 8 rules and give their renters a good place to live.

Common Fail Points in Section 8 Housing Inspections
Inspections for Section 8 housing are thorough and look at many parts of a building to make sure they meet HUD's Housing Quality Standards. There are, however, common places that property owners often forget about, which can cause inspections to fail. Drawing attention to these can help with preventative upkeep and following the rules.

- **Smoke Detectors:** A lot of the time, smoke alarms don't work, are missing, or have batteries that are dead. Check and fix all smoke alarms on a regular basis. Make sure they are in the right places, like near beds, and check them every month.

- **Window Locks:** Windows that don't have locks that work or that are painted shut often fail checks. Make sure that all of the windows can open, close, and lock properly. Paint sealing windows shut can be avoided and fixed with regular upkeep.

- **Electrical Outlet Covers:** Electrical outlet covers that are missing or broken are a typical place where things go wrong because they pose a safety risk. Replace any plug covers that are missing or broken. Check plugs often for damage or possible dangers.

- **Peeling off paint:** Painting that is peeling or chipping is common in older homes, especially paint that is made with lead. Paint should be checked and maintained regularly, especially in older buildings. Take care of any places that are peeling or chipping right away.

- **Plumbing Leaks:** Small leaks in plumbing fixtures or under sinks are often missed until the check. Check all plumbing parts, pipes, and places under the sink for leaks or water damage on a regular basis.

- **Not having enough air flow:** This is a problem because bathrooms and kitchens can get damp and moldy if they don't have enough air flow. Make sure that all of the ventilation devices work. The windows and vent fans should be able to open and close.

- **Tripping Hazards:** Tripping hazards* can be loose carpeting, uneven floors, or paths that are blocked off. Fix any carpeting that isn't level, make sure the floors are level, and make sure the walkways are clear.

- **Problem with windows:** Windows that are stuck, won't open, or have broken panes are typical problems. Make sure that all of the windows can be opened and are not broken. Fix any problems that keep windows from opening and replace any broken panes.

- **Door Locks That Won't Open or Close:** - An issue is that external doors with broken or missing locks can fail an inspection because of safety concerns. Make sure that all of the locks on the outside doors work properly by checking them all and replacing or fixing any that don't.

- **Blocked Egress:** Exits that are blocked or hard to get to can be very dangerous. Make sure that all of the doors are clear and easy to get to.

Taking care of these common problems can make it much more likely that you will pass a Section 8 check. Regular care and proactive checks are important to make sure that a building not only passes inspection but also gives tenants a safe, secure, and comfortable place to live. People who own property should be aware of these problems that could happen and act quickly to fix them.

Success Tips: Ways to Pass Section 8 Home Inspections
It is very important for property owners to pass the first Section 8 housing review in order to quickly rent out their homes and make sure they meet HUD's Housing Quality Standards. Here are some ways to focus on preventative repair and knowing what inspectors want:

- **Know what the inspection criteria are:** Learn about HUD's Housing Quality Standards. Look over the inspection checklist ahead of time to know what the testers will be looking for.
- **Do Pre-Inspection Checks:** Find problems and fix them before the real inspection. Do what it says on the HUD guide and do your own inspection. Take care of any possible weak spots.

- **Schedule regular maintenance:** Regular maintenance stops small problems from getting worse. Set up a regular maintenance plan for the whole property, including the plumbing, electrical systems, heating, and the building's structure.

- **Pay Attention to Safety and Health:** Inspectors give safety and health problems the most attention. Make sure that there are smoke alarms, carbon monoxide detectors, and fire extinguishers in the building and that they work. Look for dangers like wires that are sticking out or fences that aren't attached properly.

- **Check Plumbing and Heating Systems:** The plumbing and heating must work for the inspection to pass. Check all of the plumbing systems for leaks and to make sure they work right. Make sure the heating system works and is safe.

- **Make Sure There Is Enough airflow:** There must be enough airflow, especially in bathrooms and kitchens. Make sure all of the air fans and ventilation systems are working right.

- **Take care of cosmetic issues:** Even if they are small, cosmetic issues can cause inspections to fail. Fix broken hardware, paint that is peeling off, and damaged floors. Make sure the house looks nice and is clean.

- Look at the windows and doors to make sure they work. This is very important for safety and protection. Make sure all of the doors and windows can open, close, and lock properly. Fix any parts that are broken.

- **Pest Control:** If there are signs of infestations, the check may fail. Take regular steps to get rid of pests and deal with any signs of infection right away.

- **Documentation and Compliance:** It is very important to have the right paperwork, especially for older homes. Keep track of all the repairs, upkeep, and inspections that happen because of lead paint or other dangers.

- **Interact with Inspectors:** Getting along well with inspectors can be helpful. During the review, be there and ask questions to show that you are serious about keeping the property in good shape.

Final Thoughts

A lot of the time, passing a Section 8 housing inspection depends on how well you prepare and how well you understand the inspection standards. Focusing on safety and health, doing regular maintenance, and paying close attention to details can make passing on the first try much more likely. By using these tips, landlords can make sure that their homes not only meet HUD requirements but also offer tenants a safe, comfortable, and attractive place to live. As this chapter comes to a close, it's important to think about all the important things we've talked about in this chapter about Section 8 housing checks and the standards that HUD requires. For investors moving into this area, knowing these rules isn't just about following the law or making money; it's about a greater commitment to building good homes.

Just think about what it would be like for your kids to live in one of these homes. As a powerful way to look at your investment, this thought experiment is more than just a thought exercise. When you take care of and handle your Section 8 properties, you should treat them with the same level of care, attention to detail, and dedication to safety and comfort that you would give your own family.

Putting money into Section 8 housing isn't just a business move; it's a chance to make a real difference in the lives of families who depend on these programs. Making sure that your houses not only meet but also go beyond the HUD standards is more than just passing inspections; it's making homes.

Don't forget that your home will be a place where people make and treasure memories.

This method looks at more than just the property's physical features. It's about giving the tenants a feeling of community and belonging. Care and responsibility should guide investors when they look at their homes. This makes the community healthier and more stable. This point of view not only raises the investment's value, but it also makes the lives of the people who live in these places better.

As you start or continue your journey as a Section 8 housing investor, keep in mind that the choices and actions you take have a big effect. The homes you build can help families do well, give kids a safe place to grow, and make the neighborhood a place where people feel valued and accepted.

Finally, when investing in Section 8 housing, think about the level of care you would want for your own family. In this way, you're not just building homes; you're also building futures, making communities stronger, and showing what a big difference a careful, caring investment can make. This way of thinking will make you stand out as an investment and as someone who wants to make society better and more open to everyone.

CHAPTER 6
Handling Applications, Picking Tenants, and Working Together with Case Workers

W e're glad you're here. In Chapter 6, we'll talk about how to manage Section 8 investments in Buffalo, NY. For investors, this chapter is meant to help them understand the complicated Section 8 housing program by giving them tips on how to handle applications, choose renters, and work with caseworkers. Understanding the ins and outs of Section 8 housing is becoming more and more important for buyers who want to make money in Buffalo's real estate market.

In this chapter, we will talk about the growing need for Section 8 housing in Buffalo and what it means for investors We'll talk about how fair market rent (FMR) affects investment choices and how important it is for setting rental prices. Understanding FMR isn't just about following the rules; it's also about getting a feel for the local housing market and making sure that your business plans are in line with that.

Tenant screening turns out to be an important part of managing Section 8 homes. We will talk about how important it is for investors to do thorough background checks, verify income, and follow fair housing laws. This way, investors can be sure that the tenants they choose are not only qualified for the program but also trustworthy and responsible.

We will also talk about how important caseworkers are to the Section 8 program. These professionals are very important for clients because they make sure that the program's rules are followed. Building strong connections with caseworkers can make managing Section 8 properties a lot easier, from finding good tenants to checking on the properties.

This chapter will also show you a number of online tools and sites that can help you learn more about the Section 8 market. These tools are necessary to keep up with changes to policies, market trends, and investment possibilities in Buffalo, NY.

You'll know how to handle the Section 8 housing market in Buffalo and have all the tools and information you need to make a good investment by the end of this chapter. This chapter will help you do well in this unique and satisfying part of the real estate market, no matter how much experience you have as an investor or how new you are to Section 8 housing.

1. **Understanding the Demand:** There are a lot of applications for Section 8 housing in big cities because there aren't enough homes to go around. In places like Buffalo, NY, where real estate is really taking off, for example, it's normal to get over 100 applications for just one property listing. This high demand shows how important it is for Section 8 renters to have good property management and screen potential tenants. Investors can do well in the Section 8 rental market if they know how to meet the high demand for housing through Section 8 in growing areas and use good tenant screening and property management techniques. This strategy not only guarantees a steady flow of rental income, but it also helps their real estate business portfolio stay stable and grow.

Fair market rent (FMR) is another important consideration in real estate investing, especially for people who are in Section 8 or other government-funded housing programs. You may be wondering why I'm discussing FMR in the middle of demand analysis! The reason is to understand and forecast demand and supply efficiently. It is extremely important to understand FMR, which is the name of the rent estimates made by HUD, the U.S. Department of Housing and Urban Development. The most that a government program will pay for privately owned rental units in a certain area is based on these figures. Investors need to understand FMR for a number of reasons:

- **Setting realistic goals:** The FMR tells us how much the government will pay for rental units in a certain place. On the other hand, it's important to remember that the rent paid is usually only 75% to 90% of the FMR. This information helps owners set reasonable goals for the rental income they might get.

- **Investment Planning and Analysis:** Investors who are thinking about buying homes through Section 8 or similar programs need to understand FMR in order to make correct financial plans and investment analyses. Investors can figure out potential returns, decide if a property is a good investment, and make smart choices about property purchases when they know the FMR.

FMR analysis will make your investment more attractive, ensuring a good rate of return.

- **How to Deal with Rent Increases:** FMR can change every year depending on how the market is doing and how much money is available in the budget. Investors need to know about these changes in order to talk to housing officials about rent increases in a smart way. Because they know this, their rental income stays in line with inflation and market trends.

- **Market dynamics and property valuation:** These are both influenced by a variety of factors, including the state of the economy, the local housing market, and congressionally set spending caps. Investors need to understand these factors in order to accurately value properties and find good investment options.

- **Strategies for Keeping Renters:** In rental markets that are competitive, knowing FMR helps landlords come up with ways to keep Section 8 renters. Landlords can make sure they have a steady stream of income and lower vacancy rates by setting rents close to FMR and providing good housing.

- **Risk Reduction:** Investors who know about FMR and how to calculate it can lower the risks that come with investing in government-subsidized homes. Investors can avoid financial problems by knowing their greatest possible income and making budgets based on that.

- **Compliance and Regulations:** Another way to stay in compliance is to learn about FMR. Investors need to follow HUD rules and guidelines, and knowing FMR is part of this. Not following the rules can get you in trouble with the law and cost you money.

To sum up, FMR is an important part of investing in real

estate, especially when it comes to government-subsidized housing. Setting rent limits is based on it, and it also helps with budgeting and knowing how the market works. For investors, understanding FMR well is not only helpful; it's necessary for long-term success in real estate acquisition.

Why more people need Section 8 housing in Buffalo, NY
The need for Section 8 homes has grown a lot in Buffalo, New York, over the past few years. With the help of new data and events in the region, this document aims to give an overview of the reasons that are causing this rising demand.

The need for Section 8 housing has grown a lot because Buffalo's FMR has gone up. Because of this higher demand, the Buffalo Municipal Housing Authority (BMHA) said that a lot of people wanted to apply for its 2022 Section 8 Housing Choice Vochers.

Section 8 housing becomes more appealing to certain groups as the city grows and rental prices go up.

Low-income families in Buffalo are very interested in the Section 8 program because it is very attractive. Families in this program only have to pay 30% of their adjusted monthly income toward rent. The Buffalo Municipal Housing Authority (BMHA) takes care of the rest. Because of this financial arrangement, the program is a good choice for people who are looking for affordable housing. Data Source

After being closed for three years, the Buffalo Section 8

waitlist is now open again. This shows that the city has a big need for affordable housing. The fact that it's reopening shows that a lot of people need help with their housing. Since the waitlist was closed for a long time and then reopened not long ago, it's clear that Buffalo needs more affordable housing choices. Data Source

The COVID-19 pandemic has had a big effect on housing in Buffalo Niagara, which has caused rents to go up sharply. The housing problem in the area has gotten worse because rent prices are going up. As a clear sign of how the pandemic has affected housing affordability, the waitlist for Section 8 vouchers has grown, showing a greater need for more affordable housing choices. Data Source

There is a higher demand for Section 8 housing in Buffalo, NY. This is because FMR has gone up, the Section 8 program is becoming more appealing, the line has been reopened, and the COVID-19 pandemic has made housing more expensive. To meet this demand, we need to work together to come up with and adopt effective strategies for affordable housing.

2. **Screening methods that work well:** To handle this influx well, it's important to set up a good pre-screening method. This includes initial phone interviews and pre-screening surveys to quickly find out if applicants are a good fit, which saves time and money in the long run.

- **Tenant Screening Process:** Contrary to what most people think, Section 8 renters should have full background checks. This includes checking their income, criminal background, and history of renting places before. Section 8 requires renters to provide a lot of paperwork, which can help landlords figprocesses:how reliable they are. But landlords shouldn't just rely on Section 8's screening process; they should also do their own checks to make sure the tenants are good.

- **Income Verification:** One of the good things about renting to Section 8 renters is that their income is checked. Section 8 bases rent on 30% of the renter's income, which makes sure that the rental income is steady and reliable. This method helps landlords plan their finances and lowers the chance that rent will not be paid.

- **Taking Care of Evictions and Criminal Records:** A common misunderstanding is that Section 8 renters can't have a criminal record or have been kicked out of their previous homes. In fact, Section 8 does take people with certain types of felonies as tenants, and being evicted in the past does not automatically rule them out. To avoid surprises and make sure they are comfortable with the tenant's past, landlords should check these things on their own.

Criteria and Process for Picking Out Tenants

Screening possible tenants to make sure they are reliable and able to pay their rent is an important part of the leasing process. This means checking the tenant's income, usually with pay stubs or tax returns, to make sure they can regularly pay rent, which shouldn't be more than 30% of their monthly income. Checking their credit and rental records can also tell you about how responsible they are with money and how they've dealt with landlords in the past. To avoid discrimination, it is important to follow the law, like the Fair Housing Act. This includes getting permission for background checks. Lastly, when illegal background checks are done, they must be relevant and follow fair housing rules. This makes sure that they are used correctly in the decision-making process. While choosing the right tenant for your property, you may choose these verification process;

1. **Verification of Income:** Verification of income is an important part of tenant screening to make sure the tenant can regularly pay rent. Usually, pay stubs or tax returns are looked at to do this. It's important to remember that the rent shouldn't be more than 30% of the tenant's monthly income.

2. **Credit and Rental History:** Credit reports show that you are responsible with money and can pay your rent on time. The rental background of a person gives you information about how they've dealt with landlords and rental properties in the past.

3. **Legal Compliance:** It's important to follow the Fair Housing Act and other anti-discrimination laws when screening tenants to make sure you don't break any rules. This includes getting written permission for background checks and giving tenants copies of these records.

4. **Criminal Background Checks:** When doing criminal background checks, it's important to make sure they are relevant and follow fair housing rules. Only relevant criminal background should be used to decide who to rent or not.

3. **Use online tools:** The Department of Housing and Urban Development and local Public Housing Authorities (PHAs) websites are useful sources of information. In order to make the application process easier, they provide websites where people looking for Section 8 housing can find it and for property managers to list their available units.

Using online resources is important for investors who want

to learn more about Section 8 housing opportunities so they can make smart choices and manage their money well. The Department of Housing and Urban Development (HUD) and local Public Housing Authorities (PHAs) offer useful online resources and tools to help buyers understand how Section 8 investments work. Here are some online tools that are good for investors:

- **HUD's Official Website:** This is the best place for investors to find the latest government housing policy updates and information on Section 8 program rules and regulations. It's very important to know about the legal and financial parts of investing in Section 8 housing.

- **Local PHA Websites:** Each PHA website, like the official Buffalo Municipal Housing Authority (BMHA) website along with the Rental Assistance Corporation of Buffalo (RACB), has information that is specific to that region, which is important for buyers to know in order to understand how the markets work and what the rules are in each area. These websites often have listings for business opportunities and information about how much Section 8 housing people in the area need.

- **GoSection8.com for Landlords:** Investors can also use this platform; it's not just for renters. It lets property owners list their Section 8 homes, so a lot of people who might want to rent them can see them. It also has tools for analyzing the market and comparing rents.

- **Real Estate Investment Forums and Groups:** Online investment groups and forums, like BiggerPockets, give owners a place to talk about Section 8 housing, share their experiences, and learn from each other.

- **Zillow Rental Manager:** Zillow is well-known for its

general real estate listings, but it also has tools for landlords to manage rental properties, even ones that are Section 8-compliant. It can help you find homes to rent and figure out what the market trends are.

- **Software for managing rental properties:** Turbotenant and Buildium are two examples of software that can help investors who are investing in Section 8 housing. These systems help with managing multiple properties, screening tenants, and making sure that rules about housing are followed.

- **Websites for real estate in Buffalo:** Buffalo real estate websites often have parts just for investment properties, including ones that are good for people who want to invest in Section 8 housing. These platforms are very helpful for finding possible investment opportunities in certain Buffalo neighborhoods or areas. They are very helpful for investors who want to get into the city's housing market, especially the affordable housing sector.

Investors can learn more about the Section 8 market, find possible investment possibilities, and better manage their properties by using these online resources. These tools give you access to important data, market trends, and neighborhood insights that you need to successfully invest in Section 8 housing.

4. Working together with case workers:

Caseworkers are very important to the Section 8 housing program because they help renters, landlords, and the housing authority work together. As part of their job, they have to make sure that both the housing units and the tenants meet the standards of the program. Based on candidates' income and other factors, caseworkers carefully consider whether they are eligible. They also check properties to make sure they meet the Department of Housing and Urban Development's (HUD) health and safety standards. Caseworkers play a big role in making the Section 8 program run smoothly by helping tenants and owners talk to each other and solve problems that might come up. Their knowledge and oversight are very important for keeping the program honest and making sure it does its job of giving people in need safe, reasonable housing. Investors and property owners in the Section 8 market may need to understand and work with caseworkers in order to get through the program smoothly, make sure renters follow the rules, and build good relationships with tenants. Case workers are there to help owners and Section 8 tenants. They play a big role in making sure that program standards are met and in making communication easier. They can help the investors in terms of;

- Getting to know case workers and building relationships with them can make managing them easier. They can be very helpful when screening tenants, inspecting properties, and dealing with renter problems.

- It's important to know that Section 8 housing comes with a lot of paperwork and frequent inspections. Working together with caseworkers can make these steps simpler.

- There are problems, like keeping the property in good shape and getting rent from tenants, but working closely with case workers can help you find answers and solutions.

Final Thought

In conclusion, getting a tenant through Section 8 in Buffalo, NY, takes a multifaceted approach that includes managing a large number of applications, screening tenants thoroughly, and building relationships with caseworkers that allow you to work together. The growing need for Section 8 housing in Buffalo shows how important it is for investors to be good at managing these things if they want to do well in this area.

It's crucial for investors to understand how the local real estate market operates, particularly the Fair Market Rent (FMR) guidelines set by HUD. It is important to understand FMR in order to set reasonable rental income goals, make smart business choices, and follow the rules. It's also a big part of analyzing the market and figuring out how much a house is worth. This helps buyers find good deals and lower their risks.

Another important part of being a successful Section 8 investor is screening tenants well. In order to follow fair housing rules, this means verifying income, checking credit and rental histories, and doing criminal background checks. This level of thorough screening makes sure that only reliable tenants are chosen, which leads to stable rental income and fewer empty units.

Caseworkers play a very important part in the Section 8 program that can't be stressed enough. They play a significant role in ensuring that both renters and housing units adhere to program standards. Getting along well with caseworkers can make it easier to screen tenants, check properties, and deal with tenant problems, which makes managing Section 8 properties easier.

It's also important for buyers to use online tools and resources, like HUD's website, local PHA websites, and real estate platforms. These tools help investors make smart choices by giving them useful information about the Section 8 market, making it easier to list properties, and letting them analyze the market.

Most of the time, investing in Section 8 housing in Buffalo, NY, depends on knowing what the market wants, following the rules, checking tenants well, and working together with caseworkers. By getting good at these things, investors can take advantage of the Section 8 market's possibilities and build a stable and growing real estate portfolio in this exciting city.

CHAPTER 7
Common Misconceptions versus Realities
Maintaining Properties: The Key to Long-Term Success

The real estate business is always changing, and Section 8 housing in Buffalo, NY, is one area where a lot of inaccurate information keeps people from entering this lucrative market. Using a mix of facts and real-life examples, this chapter tries to bust these myths and show what Section 8 investments can really do. Some people think that Section 8 properties are always in bad shape. To dispel this idea, I'll show you how smart investments and regular upkeep can turn properties into desirable renters, just like I did with a three-bedroom house in Lovejoy. We'll also talk about the idea that Section 8 renters aren't reliable by giving examples of tenants who have paid their rent on time and stayed in their homes for a long time. We'll also clear up the myth that investing in Section 8 properties doesn't make money by showing how competitive rental rates, high demand, and big tax breaks can all help you make more money. This chapter isn't just a list of facts; it's also a story that shows how important it is to understand and use the Section 8 program. It also shows that investment in Section 8 housing can be both socially responsible and financially rewarding if you do it the right way. Don't forget that this information is just that—information. It shouldn't be used instead of getting professional legal or tax help.

If a right action is done wrong,
it is the method that is to blame,
not the action itself.

A lot of people have the wrong ideas about real estate business, especially when it comes to Section 8 housing in Buffalo, NY. These misunderstandings can stop people who want to invest from looking into this profitable market. With facts and real-life examples, this chapter tries to dispel these myths and show what Section 8 investments are really like and what they can do.

- **Misconception 1: Properties in Section 8 are always in bad shape**
  The truth is: Some Section 8 homes may need fixes, but a lot of them are well taken care of and in good shape. As an investor, you can pick the buildings you want to buy and keep them in good shape.

  As an example, a three-bedroom house in Lovejoy that I own was in bad shape when I first bought it. You can turn these properties into desirable rentals with the right investment. After renovations, it not only passed the Section 8 inspection, but it also became a popular renter.

  Section 8 housing is an important part of the U.S. Department of Housing and Urban Development (HUD). Its goal is to help low-income families, the elderly, and people with disabilities find decent, safe, and clean housing. This program is very important to the housing market in Buffalo, NY, but there are a lot of false ideas about it, especially about the quality of the homes that are eligible.

HUD standards are not to hinder your progress. They will eventually be great for your property's health.

HUD sets Housing Quality Standards (HQS) to make sure that all Section 8 rental homes meet basic health and safety standards. These standards cover a lot of ground, including bathrooms, areas where food is prepared, heating, lead-based paint, access, the site and neighborhood, cleanliness, smoke alarms, and more.

In Buffalo, a home must pass an HQS check before it can be rented to a Section 8 member. This inspection is very thorough and makes sure that the house is safe to live in. Some of the things that are considered are the property's general condition, its plumbing and electrical systems, and how safe and useful they are.

There is a big need for Section 8 housing in Buffalo, and the local government, like the Buffalo Municipal Housing Authority, is very important in running these programs. It's not easy to find exact numbers on how many homes in Buffalo pass the HQS on the first inspection, but it's clear that these standards are important for keeping the quality of life at a basic level.

Buffalo landlords have to make sure their properties meet these standards, which can mean a lot of work on repairs and care. However, this also opens up a chance. Properties that regularly meet or exceed HQS are more likely to get reliable tenants who will stay for a long time, which can help you make a steady rental income.

For tenants, HQS guarantees that they will live in a safe and healthy place. When Section 8 homes are well taken care of, they can help make neighborhoods better places to live and keep them stable.

If owners in Buffalo, NY, want to rent to Section 8 tenants, they need to know about and follow the Housing Quality Standards. You can't say enough good things about giving a good living to a group of people who need it the most, even though it comes with some problems. As an investor, keeping homes up to these standards is not only the law, but also a key to long-term success in the Section 8 housing market.

- **Misconception 2: Section 8 tenants can't be trusted.**
A common misunderstanding among landlords and the public is that Section 8 renters are never reliable or good for anything. People often think this way because they are biased or don't know much about the Section 8 program. It means that these renters are more likely to not pay their rent, damage property, or act in a way that bothers other people.

As an example: some of my tenants have been with me for years, which shows how reliable they are and how stable they are for my business portfolio. One of the best things about renting to Section 8 renters is that they will always pay their rent on time. I have one of the tenants who pay even before the end of the month, whereas ideally she is supposed to pay by the 7th of the following month. The government subsidizes some of the rent and pays it straight to the landlords. This makes it less likely that rent will be missed or paid late.

A lot of people who live on Section 8 are looking for safe, long-term housing. This need for security often leads to longer leases, which is good for landlords because it lowers the number of moves. On average, Section 8 tenants prefer to stay 10 years on one property.

People who live in Section 8 apartments must follow strict rules set by the HUD. Tenants have a strong reason to stay in good standing because if they don't follow the rules, like causing damage to property or breaking the law, they could lose their housing grant.

Lenders can still check out Section 8 renters the same way they would any other tenant. Landlords can use this method to look at rental records, credit scores, and other relevant data to make sure they are hiring trustworthy people.

The Section 8 program helps a wide range of people and families, such as the disabled, the elderly, and families with low incomes. A lot of them are responsible people who want to live in a safe and stable

It's not true that Section 8 renters can't be trusted; this is just a stereotype. Many people who live in Section 8 apartments are actually responsible, long-term renters who value the chance to have a stable house. Successful tenancy depends a lot on how well you screen tenants and handle your property, just like any other rental agreement. Landlords can get rid of these myths and see the benefits of renting to Section 8 renters by learning about and accepting the facts about Section 8 housing.

- **Misconception 3: Section 8 investing doesn't give good returns on money.**
A common misconception among investors is that putting money into Section 8 housing doesn't pay off. The idea behind this false belief comes from beliefs about lower rental prices, possible damage to property, and the thought that managing government programs is hard.

Section 8 provides a steady and dependable flow of money. The government directly supports and pays for a sizable portion of the rent. This makes sure that payments are always made and lowers the risk of not paying the rent.

Section 8 rents are not always less than market rates, despite what most people think. Section 8 wages are often the same as or even higher than market rates in many places, like Buffalo, NY.

People really want Section 8 housing, and there are often long waiting lines. Because of this desire, vacancy rates may go down, making sure that properties consistently make money. Earlier in this book, I mentioned that after listing the property for rent, I used to get more than 100 applications. Then it comes a hard time for me to sort them out to finally choose one.

- **Misconception 4: No Tax Breaks and Other Incentives**
  Putting money into Section 8 housing can give you special tax breaks. These could include deductions for things like property taxes, maintenance costs, and other costs that come with managing land.

Because there is a high demand for Section 8 housing, owners often pay less to market and find tenants. Most of the time, it's easy to find tenants through recommendations from housing authorities. On one occasion, I did not list the property. While the house was under renovation, a section 8 tenant requested that I rent out to her. We then communicated with her case worker, and after inspection, she got the house!

Section 8 tenants often want stability, which means they stay in their homes for longer amounts of time. This lowers the costs of getting new tenants and the costs that come with it.

Case studies and data from successful Section 8 owners can show that these investments can make more money. For example, in Buffalo, NY, properties have shown good returns on investment (ROI) compared to other types of rental properties.

A common misunderstanding is that Section 8 investment doesn't give good returns on money. In fact, Section 8 properties can offer returns that are on par with or even better than regular rental properties. This is because rent payments are stable because the government backs them up, rental rates are fair, demand is high, and there may be tax benefits. Like any other investment, making money with Section 8 housing takes planning and knowing how the local market works.

The point of this explanation is to give you a full picture of the money side of Section 8 trading by dispelling the myth with facts and examples. People who want to invest in Section 8 properties should do a lot of research and think about the unique opportunities they can provide.

Please keep in mind that the information below is only meant to be informative and is not meant to be legal or tax advice. Investors should talk to their Certified Public Accountants (CPAs) or tax experts before making any choices based on this information.

Figuring out the tax benefits
Some tax breaks can make investing in Section 8 housing a much better idea, which can greatly increase the return on investment (ROI). These tax breaks not only encourage landlords to offer affordable homes, but they also make financial sense for investors in real estate in general.

Important Tax Breaks:

- **Depreciation of Property:** Property depreciation is one of the most important tax breaks for real estate owners. This lets owners deduct a part of the cost of the property over the IRS-defined useful life. This benefit can be used to lower taxable income each year by offsetting rental income.

- **Maintenance and Repairs:** You can deduct the costs of keeping and fixing up a Section 8 property from your taxes. This includes the prices of regular upkeep, repairs, upgrades, and renovations that are needed to meet Housing Quality Standards (HQS). On the other hand, you may get compensation from Section 8 for major remodel. In one of the incidents, I had to remodel the bathroom for my tenant as she was facing post surgery complications. Since that remodel was not a routine task, Section 8 compensated for the majority of the portion through rent increase.

- **Travel Expenses:** If you need to travel to and from your Section 8 properties for business reasons, you may be able to deduct these costs. This covers costs like gas, taxis, hotels, and meals while traveling for business.

- **Insurance and property taxes:** The amount of the premiums paid for property insurance and property taxes is tax-deductible. All rental units, including Section 8 housing, have to pay these costs.

- **Interest on loans:** You can deduct the interest you pay on mortgages or loans used to buy or fix up Section 8 homes. This can be a big tax break, especially in the beginning when interest rates are high and the mortgage is still being paid.

- **Legal and Professional Fees:** You can deduct the fees you pay for legal help, property management, accounting, and other professional services that are tied to running your Section 8 property.

The opportunity to increase ROI: These tax breaks can make the net return on your Section 8 investment a lot higher. By lowering your taxable income, they lower your tax bill, which makes your business more profitable overall.

Investing in Section 8 housing is a special way to get a higher return on your money because you can get tax breaks. These deductions, which include things like property taxes and upkeep fees, can lower your taxable income by a large amount, which lowers your total tax bill. This lower tax rate directly means that your business will make more money.

I've noticed that many investors I know list their properties under their personal names rather than under LLCs. If they had chosen to hold these properties through LLCs, they could have potentially benefited from significant tax advantages.

- **The Role of LLCs in Tax Planning:** It can be a smart move to set up different limited liability companies (LLCs) for each property. There is a formal separation between the business and the investor's personal assets when they form an LLC. This separation protects you from responsibility and may have big tax benefits.

- **Deductions and Responsibilities:** Each LLC can get its own set of tax breaks based on its own land. In this group are things like mortgage interest, repairs, insurance payments, and more. The separate entity framework also limits your personal liability if there are legal problems with a certain property.

- **Compliance with Tax Laws:** With an LLC, you can choose how you are charged. Depending on how they are set up and what they want, they can be treated as a sole proprietorship, a partnership, or a company. This gives tax planners the freedom to make the best plans for each property based on its unique circumstances.

- **Importance of Keeping Good Records:** To get the most tax breaks, it's important to keep careful records of all the costs that come with each property. This includes bill payments, bank records, receipts, and any other proof of spending.

- **Have separate bank accounts:** If you have more than one LLC, it's important to keep separate business records for each one. This split makes it easier to file taxes and keeps track of expenses more clearly.

- **Navigating Tax Laws with Professional Help:** Tax laws can be hard to understand, especially when they come to real estate and business properties. Talking to a real estate-specific tax expert can give you a lot of useful information and personalized help. You should have a good CPA to be successful in real estate.

- **Optimization and Compliance:** A tax expert can help you make sure you are following all IRS rules and getting all the tax breaks you are entitled to. They can help you figure out the best ways to set up your accounts and get the most tax breaks.

You can get much better returns on your Section 8 property

investments by using LLCs strategically, keeping very good records, and getting professional tax help. Using these tax breaks not only makes sure you follow the rules, but it also helps your real estate business make more money. This method shows how important it is to have a well-thought-out business plan when it comes to Section 8 housing. The big tax breaks that come with investing in Section 8 properties can make them a lot more appealing. By learning about and taking advantage of these tax breaks, investors can increase their return on investment (ROI) while also giving low-income families the safe homes they need. This is a win-win situation for everyone, hitting the perfect balance between being responsible with money and helping others.

Taking care of properties is important for long-term success
Taking good care of your Section 8 properties is very important if you want your investment to last and make money. Regular maintenance not only makes sure that Section 8 rules are followed, but it also raises the value of the property and makes tenants happier. It is very important to use a proactive maintenance approach. As an example, regular maintenance checks on my buildings have cut the cost of emergency repairs by 24% and made it easier to keep tenants.

Section 8 tenants can be good for owners, despite what most people think. They often look for long-term housing that will give them security and regular occupancy. People who live in Section 8 apartments are not more likely to damage property than other renters. Like any group, the level of tenants varies, and it's important to do a good job of screening them.

One of the best things about renting to Section 8 renters is that it can help you stay financially stable. The government guarantees some of the rent, which lowers the risk of income changes. This is especially appealing when the economy is unclear.

Getting Rid of Stereotypes
It's important to fight against myths and learn how Section 8 housing really works. A lot of landlords have found success and happiness in renting good homes to this group of people. Investors can make money with this less risky business option by keeping properties in good shape and building good relationships with tenants. In my portfolio, I have both Section 8 and non-Section 8 tenants. I hardly get any issues from Section 8 tenants. Whereas for non-Section 8 tenants, several times I get delayed or even no rent payments.

The View from Buffalo, NY
The need for Section 8 homes in Buffalo creates a one-of-a-kind chance for investors. Investors can find a niche that has both a

social effect and a financial return by focusing on this market. When investing in Section 8 properties, it's important to keep an open mind and have a plan. Section 8 housing investments are more than just a good business move; they're also a chance to make a difference while making money. Investors can find a lot of great chances in the real estate market if they can bust some myths about Section 8 tenants and learn the truth about them.

Final Thought

As this chapter comes to a close, it's clear that Section 8 housing, especially in Buffalo, NY, is misunderstood. Misconceptions can keep buyers from seeing the real value of the market. Throughout this chapter, we have worked through a number of common myths and replaced them with facts and personal situations that show them to be false. As you go through these false beliefs, you'll see that, despite what most people think, Section 8 properties can be well-kept, attractive, and profitable investments.

With the right method, properties that are in bad shape can be fixed up and turned into desirable rentals. This shows that the state of Section 8 housing is often a result of the landlord's dedication rather than a defect in the program itself. Some people say that Section 8 tenants are not reliable, but examples of tenants who pay their rent on time and consistently, who stay in the same place for a long time, and who want stable housing show that tenants who are reliable are often the result of careful screening and good property management.

People's false beliefs about how profitable Section 8 investments are have also been busted. This shows how competitive rental rates, high demand, and big tax breaks can greatly increase investment returns. The goal of this chapter was not only to clear up any confusion but also to show how to spend wisely in Section 8 housing. In this industry, success is possible with careful management, market knowledge, and following the rules. This shows how important it is to have a well-informed, strategic approach.

This chapter basically tells people who want to invest in Section 8 housing in Buffalo, NY, to ignore the myths and see the chances it has to offer. It's an invitation to see profitable business opportunities while also doing good in the community by giving people who need it good housing. As we go on, let this chapter serve as a guide and an inspiration for you to follow the rewarding road of investing in Section 8 homes. Remember that the information here is just a starting point. Investors should talk to a professional to make sure that their plans are right for them.

CHAPTER 8
The Importance of Regular Maintenance in Section 8 Housing Investments

R eal estate owners in Buffalo, NY, have a one-of-a-kind chance to make money by investing in Section 8 housing. This chapter talks about the important parts of keeping homes up to quality standards, finding the right balance between cost and quality in property maintenance, and knowing how stable Section 8 income is.

With Section 8 housing investments, real estate owners in Buffalo, NY, are in a unique market that could be very profitable. The goal of this chapter is to break down the multifaceted approach that is needed to do well in this area. We will talk about the most important parts of maintaining properties to meet and go beyond quality standards, how to find the best balance between low cost and high quality upkeep, and how reliable Section 8 income streams are.

Taking care of homes in Buffalo's Section 8 housing market isn't just about following the rules; it's also about setting a high standard for quality. This part will talk about how important it is to do regular repairs on properties to make sure they not only meet Housing Quality Standards (HQS) but also give tenants a safe and comfortable place to live.

Finding problems quickly and fixing them can save a lot of money in the long run.

We'll talk about effective strategies for preventive maintenance and how regular upkeep can keep the property's value, avoid big repairs, and save money in the long run. This chapter will help you find and use maintenance solutions that are both cost-effective and focus on quality. It's all about finding the right balance between keeping costs low and keeping the property's style and value.

We'll talk about the idea of investing in quality changes and how they can save you a lot of money in the long run and raise the value of your home. For example, we'll look at how energy-efficient upgrades and modern renovations can do just that.

Investing in Section 8 housing with a stable income is a great way to save money because the government pays for the rent. This part will explain how this security can make a big difference, especially when the economy is changing quickly.

We'll look at the changes in demand in Buffalo, NY, and how the rising popularity of Section 8 housing can help bring down vacancy rates and make sure there is a steady flow of income. This chapter is meant to be a complete guide for real estate investors in Buffalo, NY, who want to get into the Section 8 housing market or add to their existing property. Real estate investors can get the most out of their investments by focusing on good upkeep, finding ways to save money, and taking advantage of the steady income that Section 8 provides.

Why regular maintenance is important
For you to follow the Housing Quality Standards (HQS) set by

HUD, you need to do regular repairs These rules make sure that rental homes are safe, clean, and good for people who want to live there.

- A key part of being a successful real estate investor, especially in the Section 8 housing market, is putting money into regular repairs and care. This proactive method doesn't just fix problems as they come up; it also stops problems from happening in the first place. If you do regular maintenance and checks, you can greatly lower the chance that you will need to make big, expensive repairs in the future. This includes a thorough check of the property's most important systems and structures to make sure everything is running at its best.

Important Points of Focus

- **Plumbing Vigilance:** It is very important to have regular plumbing checks. This includes looking for leaks, making sure the pipes are in good shape, and making sure all the fixtures work right. If you catch a small leak early, it might not turn into a big plumbing problem that costs a lot of money and causes problems for renters.

  Say you own a rental home for people with disabilities. During one of your regular maintenance checks, you find a small leak under the kitchen sink that doesn't seem important. It is only a slow drip, so it is simple to miss. But because you know how important it is to be careful with pipes, you decide to look into it further.

  You look at the leak and find that it's coming from a pipe part that is worn out. It's not a big deal right now, but if you don't fix it, it could cause a pipe to burst, which would flood the house and cause a lot of damage. You call a reliable plumber right away to fix the joint. The plumber agrees that it was a small problem and fixes it for a reasonable price. As long as the plumber is there, you ask them to carefully check the whole plumbing system. They make sure that everything else is in good shape by checking all the lines, fittings, and fixtures.

The repair doesn't really bother your renters because it's quick and doesn't get in the way of their daily lives. They value how quickly you responded and how well you took care of the property. If you take care of the problem quickly, you can escape a major plumbing disaster. What could have been a pricey fix that required fixing water damage, possibly getting rid of mold, and even moving tenants is now just a small fix.

Regular upkeep like this keeps the property in good shape, stopping it from falling apart and keeping its value. This is especially important in the Section 8 market, where property standards have a direct effect on how well your business does.

This shows how important it is for property managers to be careful with pipes. You can avoid costly fixes, keep your tenants happy, and keep the value of your investment high by doing regular checks and fixing problems right away. In real estate investing, this proves the saying, "A stitch in time saves nine."

- **Checks of the Electrical System:** Another important area is electrical systems. As part of regular checks, all electrical fixtures should be checked to make sure they are safe and up to code, as well as the wires and outlets. This keeps your renters safe, which is the most important thing in property management, and saves you money on repairs.

Suppose one of your Section 8 properties has some

old outlets that don't have current safety features like ground fault circuit interrupters (GFCIs). You find these when you do a regular check of the electrical system. You quickly replaced these outlets with GFCI ones when you realized the possible danger, especially in wet areas like bathrooms and kitchens. This proactive step not only makes sure that current safety codes are followed, but it also greatly improves the safety of tenants by avoiding fires or electrical shocks. Even though these updates may not seem important, they are very important for keeping your renters safe and preventing expensive electrical problems in the future.

o   **Reliability of the Structure:** It is important to check the property's structure on a regular basis. This means looking for signs of wear and tear in the base, walls, roofs, and other structural parts. Fixing small problems like roof leaks or cracks as soon as they appear can help avoid bigger issues like water damage or damage to the structure, which can be much more expensive to fix.

Advantages in the Long Run

Setting up a regular maintenance plan will pay off in the long run. For starters, it makes the property's important parts last longer, which raises the value of your investment altogether. Second, it builds a good relationship with tenants because they see that you care about keeping the place where they live safe and comfy. Lastly, it makes you look like a responsible and aggressive investor, which is very important in the Section 8 housing market, where rules about housing are closely watched. Regular upkeep isn't just a way to save money; it's an investment in the long-term health and growth of your real estate portfolio.

Properties that are well taken care of have happier tenants, which means that there is a steady flow of income. Keeping costs and quality in check when maintaining a property. Find ways to do upkeep that won't break the bank without sacrificing quality. This could mean using long-lasting materials or hiring local workers you can trust at a price you can afford.

Spending money to improve quality can save you money in the long run. For instance, upgrades that use less energy may cost more up front but save you money on your power bills over time. Fresh paint or new fixtures are two examples of regular upgrades that can keep a property looking good and raise its value over time.

Updating and maintaining Section 8 properties in Buffalo, NY, isn't just about following the rules; it's also about making a business plan that lasts and balances quality and cost. Investors can make sure their real estate deals last and be successful by focusing on regular maintenance, cost-effective property upkeep, and taking advantage of the security of Section 8 income.

Buffalo, NY's real estate market is always changing, but investing in Section 8 housing is a unique and profitable way to make money. This chapter has shown how important it is to keep properties in good shape, find a good mix between quality and cost-effectiveness in property maintenance, and make the most of the stability of Section 8 income. Regular maintenance isn't just required by law; it's also a smart way to make sure you make money and keep your tenants happy in the long run.

Maintenance that is done before it breaks, especially on plumbing and electrical systems, is very important for keeping the property's value and avoiding expensive fixes. Investors can escape big problems that could hurt their finances and reputation by taking care of small problems right away. Properties that are checked and fixed up on a regular basis not only meet Housing Quality Standards (HQS) but also provide a safe and pleasant place for renters to live, which is very important for making a real estate business last.

Regular upkeep has a lot of long-term benefits. It makes the property's important parts last longer, which raises the value of your investment as a whole. It also builds a good relationship with renters because they see a commitment to keeping the place safe and comfortable. In the Section 8 housing market, where happy tenants can mean less turnover and a steady stream of cash, this is especially important.

To sum up, quality standards and regular upkeep aren't just about following the rules; they're also about making the Section 8 housing market a sustainable and profitable business model. Investors in Buffalo, NY, can make sure their real estate deals last and be successful by focusing on regular, low-cost care and learning about how stable Section 8 income is. This chapter is meant to help buyers understand the complicated world of investing in Section 8 housing so that they can make smart choices that will pay off in the long run and help the community.

CHAPTER 9
Legal and Ethical Considerations in Section 8 Investment

Putting money into Section 8 homes in Buffalo, NY, is more than just making money; it shows a commitment to the community's well-being and morality. This chapter isn't just about following the law; it's also about accepting the big effect your investment has on people's lives and neighborhoods. Legal knowledge and morals must be combined on this trip to make sure that your business decisions are not only profitable but also good for society and make people feel better.

The most important thing for you to do as an investor is to understand and follow Section 8 rules and HUD standards. Not only should you follow the rules, but you should also understand that they are meant to protect and give power to some of the weakest people in our society. You clearly care about fairness and equality because you took the time to learn a lot about fair housing laws, rent standards, and property maintenance rules. Not only does this information protect your property, but it also makes you a better community leader and a force for good change.

Beyond the black-and-white of following the law is a wide range of moral behavior. You are more than just a property owner here; you are a guardian of houses and a builder of communities. Your moral attitude toward dealing with tenants, maintaining the property, and getting involved in the community turns buildings into homes and tenants into families. As you read this chapter, you will learn how to solve problems in an ethical way, where choices are made with empathy and understanding, taking into account both your investment goals and the real needs of your tenants.

Putting money into Section 8 homes in Buffalo, NY, is a great way to help the city grow. It's a chance to clear up some myths about Section 8 housing and show how ethical investment methods can help communities grow and thrive. This chapter isn't just about rules and strategies; it's also a plan for leaving a good legacy, where every choice you make adds to a bigger story of hope, growth, and community resilience.

As you start this journey, keep in mind that your choice to invest in Section 8 housing says a lot about your values and goals. This chapter is meant to be your guide, showing you the way to a successful, meaningful, and impactful investment job in the heart of Buffalo, NY, where legal compliance and ethical practices meet.

Legal Framework: What Section 8 Investments Are Based On

- **Get to know the Section 8 regulations**
  To be a successful Section 8 real estate investor in Buffalo, NY, it is very important to know a lot about both HUD rules and local housing authority rules. This means knowing a lot about the main parts of the Section 8 program, like who can be a renter, how much money is expected to be paid, and any Buffalo-specific rules. To make sure that housing and renter selection are done without bias, it is important to know about the Fair Housing Act. It's also important to understand the details of rent standards, such as what a fair rent amount is and how to make changes to your rent. HUD's Housing Quality Standards (HQS) govern property care. To stay in compliance, properties must be inspected regularly and maintained according to these standards. Finally, creating

a clear, unbiased, and consistent way to screen potential tenants that includes credit, rental history, and criminal background checks while also following fair housing laws is important for managing properties in the Section 8 market in a way that is both successful and moral. This thorough knowledge not only makes sure you follow the law, but it also makes you look like a responsible and knowledgeable investor who cares about the community and the well-being of your renters.

- **Norms for Inspection**
To stay in line with Section 8 rules, you need to know everything there is to know about the property inspection standards set by your Buffalo, NY, housing authority. These checks are very important to make sure that homes meet the Housing Quality Standards (HQS) that HUD requires. The HQS includes a number of factors, such as how safe, clean, and habitable the property is generally. Important parts include making sure the electricity systems work well and are safe, that there is enough heat and air flow, that the building's parts are secure and whole, and that there are no dangerous materials or conditions. The property must also have enough living room, including places to sleep, clean water, and proper systems for getting rid of trash. The local housing authority does regular checks to make sure that these standards are being met. As a Section 8 owner, it's your job to make sure that these standards are always met and that any problems are fixed right away so that you don't get fined or kicked out of the program. By understanding and following these inspection standards, you will not only be in line with Section 8 rules, but you will also show that you care

about giving your renters good housing, which will reflect well on your investment ethics and standards.

- **Fair Housing Laws:**
A big part of being an honest property manager, especially in the Section 8 housing market, is knowing and following the Fair Housing Laws. The Fair Housing Act is a very important law that stops housing discrimination based on race, color, national origin, religion, sex, family status, or disability. As an investor, you need to make sure that all present and potential tenants are treated fairly and equally, without any bias or prejudice. This means that choices about choosing tenants, setting rent prices, evicting tenants, and other parts of managing properties must not be biased.

Making accommodations for renters with disabilities is also very important. This means making sensible changes to the rental rules or the property itself to make sure that everyone can get to and live in it. For example, adding steps to make bathrooms safer and easier for people in wheelchairs to use or changing rules to allow service animals even on properties that don't allow pets are all examples of changes that could be made. These changes are not only required by law, but they also show that you care about all of your tenants and treat them with respect. This will support your investment plan in the Buffalo, NY, Section 8 market.

As a Section 8 real estate owner, one important thing to remember is that the Fair Housing Laws say you should be open to all kinds of tenants. Even though you may be focusing on Section 8 properties, keep in mind that the Fair Housing Act says you have to treat all possible tenants equally, even if they are not in the Section 8 program. This means that when you're looking for tenants, you shouldn't just choose those who have a Section 8 grant.

All applicants should be judged in the same manner, like how well they can pay rent, keep the property in good shape, and follow the rules of the lease. This method makes sure that you don't treat renters differently just because they don't have a Section 8 voucher, which is what the law says you have to do for fair housing. You are not only following the law when you use this method, but you are also building a diverse and fair community on your properties. This is an important way to show that you care about fairness and equality in the Buffalo, NY, housing market. It's also a great way to clear up any misunderstandings about Section 8 investments, which makes your investment plan more ethical.

- **Reasonable Rent:**
A key part of your business plan in Buffalo, NY, is making sure to set fair rents. Rents should be set based on the market rates for similar units in the area and should also be in line with HUD's payment guidelines. This should be done on a frequent basis. This balance makes sure that renters can afford the property and that your investment will be profitable. Key steps in this process include researching the market and keeping up with local real estate trends. It is also very important to know HUD's rules for making rent changes. Most of the time, rent can be changed when the lease is renewed or when there are big changes in the market, improvements to the property, or the median income in the area. Any suggested rent increase must, however, be fair, reasonable, and within HUD's payment limits. Additionally, it's crucial to be upfront with tenants about any rent changes and give them the time they need to comply with the law. Fair rent practices and knowing the details of rent adjustments will not only help you follow HUD's rules, but they will also help you build a stable and positive relationship with your tenants, which will help your Section 8 investments succeed in the long run.

- **Rules for maintaining and fixing up properties:**

It is very important for Section 8 property managers to understand and follow the Housing Quality Standards (HQS). To ensure that all Section 8 homes meet a certain level of safety and comfort, HUD created the Housing Quality Standards (HQS). These standards include a lot of different things, such as the basic strength of the building, making sure the water and heating systems work properly, making sure there is enough air flow, and making sure the building meets health and safety rules. You, as a property owner, are responsible for keeping your buildings in good shape all the time, not just when they are being inspected.

A big part of the Section 8 program is that the local housing authority inspects the homes on a regular basis. These checks are done to make sure that your sites are still meeting HQS. A first inspection is usually done before a tenant moves in, and then there may be one or two more inspections a year, based on the rules in the area. To make sure that your units always pass these checks, you should be proactive about property maintenance. Keeping up with maintenance problems not only helps you pass inspections easily, but it also improves the health and happiness of your tenants. By putting HQS-recommended maintenance on your homes first, you show that you care about providing good housing and protect your investment in the Section 8 program.

Your tenants are more than just renters;
they are people and families who will
make your place their home and make
memories that will last a lifetime.

Beyond Following the Law: Ethical Things to Think About

When you buy in Section 8 properties, you have the most important moral and ethical duties to the tenants. These duties are more than just following the rules; they have to do with understanding the human side of real estate investing. Your tenants are more than just renters; they are people and families who will make your place their home and make memories that will last a lifetime. A key part of ethical property management is treating people with respect and honor, no matter how much money they have. This means you promise to quickly take care of repair requests, which not only makes sure their living area is safe and comfortable but also shows that you are responsive and care about their health. Another important thing is to respect the tenant's privacy. This builds trust and shows that you value their right to a safe and quiet house. A feeling of community can also be created within your properties, which can greatly improve the quality of life for your tenants. This could mean planning events for the community, keeping public places in good shape, or just encouraging people to get along with each other. Focusing on these moral actions will not only make the lives of your renters better, but it will also help you build a long-lasting and trustworthy investment business that stands out in the Buffalo, NY, real estate market.

An important part of investing in real estate in an honest way is getting involved in your community. This is especially true in Buffalo, NY, where your Section 8 properties are situated. These activities are more than just managing property; they also involve making friends in the neighborhood. The starting point is to support neighborhood-improving projects and efforts in your area, whether it's by giving money, time, or resources. It is also important to be a part of neighborhood groups. Participate in meetings and conversations to learn about the needs and concerns of the community. This not only helps build community pride and a sense of belonging, but it also gives you useful information about how your properties and management style can better serve the area. It's important to listen to what the community has to say, whether it's about your businesses, ideas for making the area better, or worries about the neighborhood. Being open and responsive builds trust and respect. Being involved in the community in this way not only improves your image as a socially responsible investor, but it also makes the place where your tenants live more welcoming and helpful, which in turn makes the community stronger and more successful.

Adopting eco-friendly practices when handling your Section 8 properties in Buffalo, NY, is not only good for the environment, but it also makes sense for efficient property management and happy tenants. Using eco-friendly methods, like LED lighting, energy-efficient equipment, and long-lasting materials for repairs and renovations, can cut down on energy use and utility costs by a large amount. Taking this method will not only make the environment healthier, but it will also save you and your tenants money. Incorporating green spaces and promoting recycling programs can also make living better by creating a sense of community and improving people's health. People who rent homes that are good for the environment and save money are more likely to value and take care of their living space, which means fewer maintenance problems and longer lease terms. By making sustainability a priority in your property management plan, you not only show that you care about the environment, but you also make the living space more appealing and peaceful, which is good for both your investment and your renters.

Dealing with problems in an honest way is important and hard when investing in Section 8 real estate, especially in Buffalo, NY. Dealing with problems in a fair and understanding way is important for keeping a good landlord-tenant relationship and protecting your image as an honest investor. When problems appear, like maintenance issues, rent disagreements, or bad behavior from tenants, it's best to look at them from a balanced point of view. This means that you should listen to your tenants' concerns, try to understand their position, and look for solutions that are fair and good for everyone. For example, if a renter is having trouble making rent on time, you might want to work out a flexible payment plan with them that works with their budget while still protecting your investment interests. In the same way, fixing maintenance problems quickly and well not only meets the wants of your tenants but also keeps your property's value high. You are being ethical when you solve problems in a way that respects your tenants' wants and dignity. This will also help you keep them as tenants for a long time, which is very important for the success of your investment in the Section 8 market. This method not only makes sure that the law is followed, but it also builds trust and kindness, which are very important for long-term success in the real estate business.

Final Thoughts

As this chapter on the legal and moral issues involved in Section 8 investments comes to a close, it's a good idea to think about the trip you've been on. Putting money into Buffalo, NY, Section 8 properties is more than just a business move; it's a promise to improve neighborhoods and change people's lives. It's not just about how much money you make that determines your journey. It's also measured by the smiles of families who find safety in your properties, the thanks of renters who are treated with respect, and the strength of communities that grow stronger because of the moral things you do.

Because you invested money, you have a huge duty to follow not only the laws of the land but also the unspoken rules of humanity. Your dedication to doing the right thing when handling Section 8 properties is a bright spot in a field where misunderstandings are common. You've shown that it is possible to be smart about business and kind, to be good at investing, and to have a strong sense of humanity. This method doesn't just build homes; it also makes communities, supports dreams, and creates a sense of belonging.

Every decision you make and rule you enforce has an impact on people's lives. Never forget that the homes you rent out are the backdrops to your renters' life stories. They are where their happiness, hardship, and important moments happen. When you engage in an honest and responsible way, you're not just giving them a place to stay; you're giving them stability, safety, and respect. This effect goes beyond the boundaries of your properties and into the heart of Buffalo, NY, making good changes all over the area.

Take the things you learned from this chapter with you as you go on. Please let them help you continue to make business decisions that are both smart and moral. Imagine a world where your properties are known not only for making money but also for making people's lives better and communities stronger. Your journey through Section 8 investment isn't just a business deal; it's a legacy of kindness, honesty, and social duty.

Last but not least, keep in mind that you have a lot of respect as a Section 8 owner in Buffalo, NY. You have a one-of-a-kind chance to change people's lives, neighborhoods, and the story about Section 8 investments. Embrace this role with joy and a sense of purpose, knowing that every moral choice you make adds to a bigger story of hope, strength, and community change. Your story shows that having a heart for the community and being successful in business can go hand in hand.

ACKNOWLEDGMENTS

This book, the culmination of my journey and insights into Section 8 real estate investing in Buffalo, NY, would not have been possible without the support, data, and resources from various individuals and organizations.

I extend my gratitude to:

- Buffalo Federation of Neighborhood Centers (BFNC): For their insights into community initiatives, particularly the Westminster Commons project, shaping an understanding of local developments.

- Redfin: For their comprehensive data on Buffalo's housing market, offering a detailed perspective on market trends.

- PropertyShark: For providing crucial data on residential market trends in Buffalo, enhancing the book's relevance to current market dynamics.

- Zillow: For their valuable home value indices and market analysis, offering a broader view of Buffalo's real estate landscape.

- New York State Homes and Community Renewal (HCR): For information on Governor Hochul's comprehensive housing plan, reflecting state-level perspectives on housing initiatives.

- Buffalo Municipal Housing Authority: For insights into Section 8 housing specifics in Buffalo, deepening the understanding of local housing policies.

- WGRZ-TV: For their reporting on Section 8 housing developments in Buffalo, offering a real-time look at the housing situation.

- The Buffalo News: For their coverage of rent trends during the pandemic, providing context to the current real estate climate.

- Family and Friends: For their unwavering support and encouragement throughout my real estate journey and the writing of this book.

- Professional Colleagues: For their invaluable insights, advice, and shared experiences in the real estate sector, which have enriched the content of this book.

- My tenants and community members in Buffalo, NY: These stories and experiences have been a source of inspiration and learning, adding a human touch to the practical aspects of real estate investment.

- Editorial and Publishing Team: For their diligent work in refining and bringing this book to fruition, ensuring that it meets the highest standards of quality and clarity.

Thank you all for your contributions, which have been instrumental in the creation of this guide. Your collective wisdom, experience, and support have been the backbone of this endeavor.